1000 Facts Jeffrey Dahmer

Simon Speed

Contents

INTRODUCTION

The facts which follow cover all aspects of Dahmer's life and crimes. There have been many books and articles about Jeffrey Dahmer but hopefully this book will justify its existence and supply plenty of Dahmer trivia which you were not previously aware of. Be warned that some of the facts which follow are not for the faint of heart.

1000 FACTS ALL ABOUT JEFFREY DAHMER

(1) Jeffrey Lionel Dahmer was born in Milwaukee, Wisconsin, in 1960.

(2) Dahmer's mother Joyce was a Teletype Machine Instructor.

(3) Jeffrey Dahmer's chemist father Lionel taught him how to preserve animal bones when he was a boy. Dahmer would later use these skills on human bones.

(4) When he was a boy, Dahmer became very interested in taxidermy and decomposition. You might say this was rather Norman Bates.

(5) Dahmer said he first had a fantasy about killing someone when he was in high school.

(6) Jeffrey Dahmer collected insects as a kid.

(7) Dahmer was a fairly bright kid and had an IQ of 121 as an adult.

(8) Relatives of Jeffrey Dahmer say that his personality seemed to suddenly change after he had hernia surgery at the age of four.

(9) Dahmer attended Revere High School in Ohio.

(10) Jeffrey Dahmer said his necrophiliac desires began when he was fourteen. A necrophiliac is a person who is sexually excited by or attracted to dead bodies.

(11) Dahmer said that when he was eighteen he tried to steal a corpse from a graveyard but his plan was foiled because the

ground was too hard to dig up. Dahmer had read in the obituary section of the newspaper that a local teenage boy had died.

(12) It is a popular thread with many serial killers that their sexual fantasies from a young age were about people who are restrained or can't move or struggle. Social scientists say that the desire for absolute control and dominance we see in serial killers like Dahmer often stems from an unhappy childhood where they felt weak and vulnerable. Dahmer was said to be irritated when his lovers moved too much. He wanted them perfectly still. In fact, he REALLY wanted them dead.

(13) When he was growing-up, Jeffrey Dahmer once stole a mannequin from a store and kept it in his bedroom for a couple of weeks. Sadly, this mannequin only served to make him wish he had a real inert body to lie down with.

(14) Dahmer developed a drinking problem at a preposterously young age - which seemed to blight whatever potential he had.

(15) Dahmer's former classmates say you could often smell Scotch on his breath at school. He would also sometimes take a bottle of vodka to school with him.

(16) Jeffrey Dahmer's childhood home in Akron, Ohio, is still there. You can rent or buy this property. It is said the house has sometimes proved difficult to sell.

(17) Jeffrey Dahmer was apparently known as a prankster when he was at school. It seems though that he was egged on to do this and, having no real friends of his own, was eager to please whoever took an interest in him. Dahmer's pranks at school betray a desperate need for some sort of attention.

(18) Jeffrey Dahmer was an avid reader as a teenager. He was said to love reading The Lord of the Rings most of all.

(19) Dahmer played the clarinet in high school.

(20) Jeffrey Dahmer said he felt jealous of the attention given to his younger brother David when he was a boy.

(21) Jeffrey Dahmer and his brother David apparently had almost nothing in common. David was outgoing and cheerful - the complete opposite of Jeffrey Dahmer.

(22) Dahmer was gay and so all of his future victims would be men that he had picked up in bars or developed a casual friendship with. Heterosexual male killers nearly always kill women and gay male serial killers nearly always kill men.

(23) Dahmer went on a date with a girl at a prom when he was a teenager. He knew he was gay though so had no interest in making a habit of this.

(24) Bridget Geiger, Dahmer's prom date, said he was very shy and a little bit weird.

(25) Bridget Geiger said that Dahmer did not kiss her when they went to the prom. He merely shook her hand at the end of the night.

(26) During a school trip to Washington, Dahmer managed to blag permission to visit the Vice-President's office in the White House.

(27) Jeffrey Dahmer quickly abandoned Bridget Geiger at the prom and vanished. He only returned hours later to take her home.

(28) Dahmer graduated from high school in 1978.

(29) Dahmer is believed to have killed for the first time when he was eighteen. Dahmer murdered a hitchhiker named Steven Hicks he had picked up by hitting him with a barbell weight.

(30) Dahmer threw the remains of his first victim Steven Hicks in the woods in garbage bags after dissecting the body. A few weeks later, Dahmer used acid to dissolve the body of Steven Hicks and crushed whatever bones were left with a hammer.

(31) Dahmer's father paid for him to go university but he dropped out after a few months. Dahmer attended Ohio State University.

(32) After dropping out of university, Dahmer became a combat medic assistant in the 8th Infantry Division and was stationed in West Germany. It was his father who insisted that he should join the army.

(33) Two soldiers who served with Dahmer claimed that he sedated and raped them in Germany.

(34) Dahmer's army record indicates that he was an excellent marksman and skilled with guns.

(35) Dahmer's army record also indicated that he was a persistent lawbreaker. He would sometimes turn up for duty drunk. He was also reprimanded for playing his stereo too loud.

(36) Jeffrey Dahmer was eventually kicked out of the army for his drinking. He refused to participate in rehabilitation schemes designed to get him sober.

(37) After his discharge from the army and a year in Florida, Dahmer eventually ended up living with his grandmother in West Allis, Wisconsin.

(38) As a young man, Dahmer was arrested for indecent exposure to children.

(39) Dahmer had a conviction for dangerous driving as a teenager. He was caught veering over the middle of the lane.

Dahmer had bags containing the remains of Steven Hicks in the car at the time. He was amazed that the cops didn't search his car.

(40) Dahmer was briefly employed as a phlebotomist at the Milwaukee Blood Plasma Center.

(41) Jeffrey Dahmer was eventually employed at Ambrosia Chocolate Factory in Milwaukee. While working at the chocolate factory, Dahmer drugged and sexually fondled a 13-year-old boy. He was given five years' probation.

(42) At the chocolate factory, Dahmer worked the night shift for $8.75 an hour.

(43) Jeffrey Dahmer was a mixer at the chocolate factory.

(44) Dahmer was eventually fired from his job at the chocolate factory for missing shifts.

(45) In 1987, Jeffrey Dahmer woke up in the Ambassador Hotel in Milwaukee with the dead body of a man next to him. He somehow managed to get the body out of the hotel using a suitcase and took it to his grandmother's home (where Dahmer lived) so that he could dissect the body and dispose of it. Dahmer became aware that it was relatively easy to pick up young men and as he was living with just his grandmother he had a relative sort of privacy at home. The victim was Steven Walter Tuomi. This was Dahmer's second murder.

(46) In the end, Jeffrey Dahmer's grandmother, though she loved her grandson, got tired of his strange behaviour and he had to leave. Dahmer eventually moved into an apartment and his killing spree then began to spiral out of control. Jeffrey Dahmer lived at Apartment 213, Oxford Apartments—924 N. 25th street, Milwaukee, Wisconsin.

(47) Dahmer often went to a nightclub called Club 219 to find victims. Club 219 was a real gay bar in Milwaukee. Dahmer's

apartment was very close - about a ten minute cab ride away.

(48) Club 219 closed in the end. It was a combination of new rival nightclubs and the infamy of being associated with Dahmer that sunk this once profitable establishment.

(49) Dahmer would sometimes pick up victims at The Grand Avenue. This was a local Milwaukee mall which opened in 1982. The mall still exists to this day.

(50) Dahmer tends to be known as The Milwaukee Cannibal in true crime circles today.

(51) Dahmer said that he was a nervous child because there was always tension in the house between his mother and father.

(52) Dahmer's mother once suffered a nervous breakdown and is often alleged to have been an unstable person prone to eccentric behaviour. This is sometimes speculated to have had an adverse affect on Jeffrey Dahmer.

(53) Jeffrey Dahmer was always irritated by media reports or academic articles which apportioned some blame to his parents for him becoming a serial killer. Dahmer was always quick to insist that his parents were not to blame for anything.

(54) Dahmer is most famous for the fact that he would eat parts of his victims. It is very rare for serial killers to eat the flesh of their victims. This fact makes the known cannibal serial killers all the more infamous. There are not a huge amount of killers where we know for a fact that they ate parts of their victims and so verified killers who fall into this category are (unavoidably) all the more macabre and morbidly fascinating.

(55) Dr Eric Hickey, professor of forensic psychology at Walden University, estimated that around only around five to ten out of every two thousand serial killers are cannibals.

(56) Given that his victims were mostly black, it has been speculated that there was a racist motive in Dahmer's selection of victims. The evidence for this seems weak though. It seems to be more the case that Dahmer simply targeted people who were available to him in that location and transient or vulnerable. These people often turned out to be black because Dahmer lived in a black neighbourhood.

(57) Dahmer told the police that the race of his victims was unimportant to him and not a factor in why they were chosen. According to Dahmer they just in the wrong place at the wrong time.

(58) It seems highly plausible that Dahmer might have targeted black victims simply because he was sexually attracted to black men.

(59) Dahmer said the human body parts he ate tasted a lot like beef.

(60) Jeffrey Dahmer fried the body parts of his victims in a skillet before he ate them.

(61) Dahmer used a meat tenderizer to make human flesh more edible.

(62) Dahmer said that, circa 1983, he tried to use religion to fight off his desperate urge to kill and attended church a lot. It obviously didn't work.

(63) Jeffrey Dahmer said he enjoyed his time in the army and regretted the fact that his drinking got him kicked out. Dahmer said that the routines and discipline of army life helped to keep his dark thoughts and desires at bay.

(64) Dahmer briefly lived in Florida after he was booted out of the army. Dahmer said he went there because afer living in Ohio and Germany he was tired of the cold winters and wanted to go somewhere warm for a change. Dahmer did not

kill anyone while in Florida - although, as we shall see, some suspect him of killing a child while in Florida.

(65) Jeffrey Dahmer said he once planned to kill a jogger who ran past his house each day. The jogger stopped running past his house though.

(66) When Dahmer moved into his own apartment this made bringing men back and killing them much easier but it also made disposing of the evidence much harder. It was a more constrictive environment. Dahmer was soon completely lost in his own world of murder and depravity.

(67) The way Dahmer got the victims back to his apartment was to offer them money for a photo shoot or sex. They evidently didn't detect any danger from him and so took the chance to make some extra cash. Dahmer was bespectacled and mild in temperament and speech so he wasn't someone who raised obvious alarm bells or seemed dangerous.

(68) Jeffrey Dahmer's apartment was so eventually so full with victims and body parts that he put one body in the bath and had to shower over it. According to some sources Dahmer had TWO bodies in the shower in the end.

(69) Jeffrey Dahmer would sometimes get his victims handcuffed by telling them he simply wanted to take a bondage photograph.

(70) Jeffrey Dahmer said in his confession that he bought a gun once but got rid of it. He never used a gun in any of his murders. It obviously would have been impossible to shoot someone in an apartment block without attracting attention.

(71) Dahmer would often put a sedative in a coffee rum drink he gave his victims. He would then kill the victims as they slept.

(72) Dahmer told the police that his victims were all strangled

- save for one who was stabbed.

(73) Radford University's 2016 report found that 21% of serial killer victims were strangled.

(74) Dahmer set up a fake security camera at his apartment to deter unexpected visitors.

(75) Dahmer said he did not sell any jewellery or valuables belonging to his victims. Dahmer was fairly shrewd and must have known this would too risky - though he would doubtless have been happy for any extra money.

(76) Dahmer said that when he lived in Florida he ran out of money at one point and had to sleep on the beach.

(77) Dahmer had casual work in Florida. He was a cook and a cleaner.

(78) Dahmer said he got mugged once when he was sleeping rough on the beach in Florida.

(79) His heavy drinking made regular employment a constant struggle for Dahmer. It's a miracle he lasted as long as he did at the chocolate factory.

(80) There would be seventeen official victims of Dahmer in all.

(81) Jeffrey Dahmer said that after his third murder he began keeping the skulls. He would boil them in a cleaning solution.

(82) Jeffrey Dahmer said that he had an exceptionally high tolerance for alcohol and that it took a lot to get him steaming drunk.

(83) Jeffrey Dahmer said that as his victim count escalated he became much better at cutting up bodies and could do this grisly dissection task surprisingly quickly in the end.

(84) Jeffrey Dahmer's tipple of choice was rum & coke.

(85) Dahmer had a tray at the bottom of his fridge to collect the blood that dripped down from body parts.

(86) The apartment of Jeffrey Dahmer contained a big blue plastic drum of acid where three human torsos were dissolving.

(87) Dahmer once drank the spiked drink he had laced for a victim by mistake. He passed out and when he woke up the victim had robbed him and left. Naturally, Dahmer didn't bother to report the crime. The 'thief' had no idea how lucky he had been that Dahmer gave him the wrong drink by mistake.

(88) Dahmer did not own a car so the option of transporting victim parts elsewhere was not available.

(89) Dahmer skinned the entire body of one his victims. He said this took two hours.

(90) Neigbours of Jeffrey Dahmer did complain about the smell coming from his apartment several times. He apparently told them once that his freezer broke and some food went bad.

(91) Dahmer is a suspect in the 1981 murder of a six year-old boy named Adam Walsh in Hollywood, Florida in 1981. Adam was found decapitated two weeks after he went missing. Jeffrey Dahmer lived in Florida at the time of this awful murder and decapitation was part of his usual MO. There is some circumstantial evidence which possibly places Dahmer at the scene of this crime. A serial killer named Otis Toole confessed to Adam's murder although he later backtracked on this confession. It is impossible to say for sure either way but the general perception is that Dahmer probably wasn't involved in Adam's death. Dahmer was questioned about Adam Walsh by the police and denied he had anything to do with this dreadful murder.
(92) Although he drank a lot Dahmer said he was never really

into drugs.

(93) Jeffrey Dahmer said his biggest problem in life was always a lack of any set goal or direction. As a consequence of this he always felt rudderless and drifting through life with no plan or motivation.

(94) Dahmer said he experimented with trying to mummify the head of one of his victims.

(95) Jeffrey Dahmer often used a handsaw to cut up his victims.

(96) Dahmer frequented local gay bathhouses and would drug other patrons so that he could sexually abuse them.

(97) Jefffrey Dahmer lived in a rough part of Milwaukee that had plenty of crime and a notoriously smelly sewer problem. This is the only explanation for why the noises and smells from his apartment didn't trigger more curiosity in his neighbours.

(98) Jeffrey Dahmer took numerous polaroids of his victims when they were dead.

(99) Dahmer played a bit of tennis at school but he didn't stick at it for very long.

(100) Believe it or not, Marvel star Jeremy Renner played Jeffrey Dahmer is a 2002 film simply called Dahmer. The movie got decent reviews.

(101) Jeffrey Dahmer was six foot tall.

(102) Jeffrey Dahmer had blue eyes.

(103) Dahmer owned a large hunting knife with a rubber grip. He would often use this knife as part of the process of dissecting a body.

(104) Jeffrey Dahmer owned a computer but he rarely used it. At the time of his capture he was actually planning to sell it.

(105) Dahmer sometimes disposed of parts of his victims in the garbage to get them out of the apartment. Amazingly, these were never discovered. Dahmer attributed this to the fact that he wrapped them up very tightly.

(106) Jeffrey Dahmer said he killed his victims so that they would never be able to leave him.

(107) Dahmer used a black nylon strap to strangle many of his victims.

(108) After he killed a victim, Dahmer would usually not dissect them for a couple of days. He did this because he wanted the corpse to have sex with while it was still 'fresh'.

(109) Dahmer claimed that he gave his victims sleeping pills before strangulation because he didn't want them to suffer. He wanted their death to be quick and unexpected. Dahmer wanted the victims to be oblivious to their predicament.

(110) Dahmer's known victims were - Steven Hicks, 18 years old, June 18, 1978, Steven Tuomi, 25 years old, Nov 20, 1987, James Doxtator, 14 years old, Jan 16, 1988, Richard Guerrero, 22 years old, March 24, 1988, Anthony Sears, 24 years old, March 25, 1989, Raymond Smith, 32 years old, May 20, 1990, Edward Smith, 27 years old, June 1990, Ernist Miller, 22 years old, Sept, 1990, David Thomas, 22 years old, Sept 24, 1990, Curtis Straughter, 17 years old, Feb, 1991, Errol Lindsey, 19 years old, April 7, 1991, Tony Hughes, 31 years old, May 24, 1991, Konerak Sinthasomphone, 14 years old, May 26, 1991, Matt Turner, 20 years old, June 30, 1991, Jeremiah Weinberger, 23 years old, July 5, 1991, Oliver Lacy, 24 years old, July 15, 1991, and Joseph Bradehaft, 25 years old, July 19, 1991.

(111) The victim that Dahmer stabbed was Ernist Miller.

Dahmer said he stabbed Miller because this victim was a powerful man and Dahmer didn't think he'd be capable of strangling him (as was his usual MO).

(112) The murder of Ernist Miller was so bloody that there were still blood stains on Dahmer's bedroom wall when he was arrested.

(113) Dahmer was always naked when he dismembered his victims. Dahmer said he did this not for kinky reasons but because he wanted to avoid getting blood or cleaning chemicals on his clothes.

(114) Jeffrey Dahmer tried to disguise the smell in his apartment by venting it with a fan. One imagines that Dahmer was always fighting a losing battle trying to mask the foul odours coming from his apartment.

(115) Dahmer told the police that human flesh was very tender to eat.

(116) Dahmer said that when he killed someone this only satisfied him for a few months. After that the urge to kill again returned stronger than ever.

(117) Jeffrey Dahmer said that when he tried to dig up the body in the graveyard he was attacked by a dog.

(118) Dahmer said he was surprised not to get caught after he killed his first victim. He said that being an undetected serial killer was easier than he expected.

(119) Jeffrey Dahmer poured acid into the head of a victim named Konerak Sinthasomphone. Sinthasomphone escaped and wandered the streets in a daze. Tragically, some policemen who found Sinthasomphone then took him back to Dahmer's apartment after Dahmer told them Sinthasomphone was his intoxicated boyfriend.

(120) Dahmer's neighbour Sandra Smith had alerted the police

to Konerak Sinthasomphone wandering the street in a daze. The police officers in this incident were highly lackadaisical because they didn't even bother to do a background check on Dahmer or take a proper look in his apartment. They just handed the victim back to him and left.

(121) John A. Balcerzak and Joseph P. Gabrish were the bungling police officers who handed the dazed and confused victim Konerak Sinthasomphone back to Jeffrey Dahmer and certain death. They were dismissed from the police after an investigation but then appealed and got reinstated.

(122) John A. Balcerzak and Joseph P. Gabrish, the police officers who tragically handed victim Konerak Sinthasomphone back to Jeffrey Dahmer, were caught on radio making homophobic comments and joking about how they had reunited 'lovers' after the incident.

(123) Dahmer was so crazy that he thought if he injected acid or boiling water into a victim's brain they would become a compliant slave for him.

(124) Jeffrey Dahmer told the police that it takes about an hour to boil a head.

(125) Dahmer said he used Soilex to boil heads.

(126) Dahmer said that sometimes he would dissolve bones in acid and flush them down the toilet.

(127) There were eleven skulls in Dahmer's apartment when he was captured.

(128) Dahmer said he had no gay encounters while he was in the army. He said he was propositioned by a sergeant though.

(129) Dahmer kept a portion of a victim's arm in his fridge with a view to eating it later. He never got around to this though because he was arrested.

(130) The Hedonistic serial killer will murder purely for their own pleasure. The gratification can come from the financial rewards of killing (like stealing money and valueless from victims) but the main motivation for this sort of killer is sexual satisfaction. There are many examples of this sort of killer. Jeffrey Dahmer is often classified as a Hedonistic killer because he lured male victims to his apartment and then sedated them to satiate his warped sexual fantasies. Dahmer had strange and unfathomable urges and desires which he couldn't stop himself from fufilling - no matter how horrific and harrowing they were. He couldn't control himself.

(131) The police found that Jeffrey Dahmer had extensive security at his apartment. He had a complex series of locks and an alarm system.

(132) The British necrophile serial killer Dennis Nilsen ended up in an identical situation to Jeffrey Dahmer. They both ended up trapped in a small apartment festooned with body parts that they couldn't dispose of.

(133) If you'd lived next to Jeffrey Dahmer you would probably have had no idea that he was a serial killer. The ability of serial killers to appear fairly normal to those around them has been described as the 'mask of sanity'.

(134) Dahmer said that he always tried to keep his apartment tidy because this made him seem more normal and less suspicious.

(135) Dahmer liked to paint human skulls because he thought this made them look fake and they would be less suspicious if discovered.

(136) Dahmer purchased the spray paint for the skulls from a local art shop.

(137) The police discovered that Dahmer had a crude illustration depicting the 'altar' he planned to construct in his

apartment. Dahmer planned to use the skulls and skeletons of his victims for this macabre shrine.

(138) Jeffrey Dahmer refused to eat people who had tattoos.

(139) Jeffrey Dahmer said he ate parts of his victims because he wanted them to always be a part of him.

(140) Jeffrey Dahmer would offer sandwiches for neighbours in his apartment building. It is therefore possible that his neighbours might have unwittingly eaten human flesh.

(141) Dahmer said he first ate human flesh purely as an 'experiment' but it became sexually exciting for him to do this in the end.

(142) Jeffrey Dahmer was captured when a man named Tracy Edwards managed to escape the handcuffs Dahmer had put on him and go and fetch some police officers.

(143) Dahmer had two hands and human genitalia in his kettle when the police searched his apartment. You definitely wouldn't want a cup of coffee from Dahmer.

(144) One of the police officers described Dahmer's apartment as like entering a real life horror museum. It was very grim and disturbing.

(145) The police found a complete skeleton in Jeffrey Dahmer's filing cabinet and three human heads in the fridge.

(146) Jeffrey Dahmer's confession to the police started at 1-30am and ended at 7-15am.

(147) During his lengthy police confession, Dahmer had five cups of coffee and two cans of Coke.

(149) At the end of his police confession Dahmer asked the police detectives if they would sit with him a bit longer so he

could discuss his offences some more. He seemed to have a desperate need to get everything off his chest.

(150) When he was captured, Dahmer told the police that he hadn't seen his parents or younger brother for years. This wasn't strictly true though. His father and stepmother had visited his apartment and Dahmer attended family Thanksgiving dinners.

(151) The police found a hypodermic needle and an electric drill in Dahmer's apartment.

(152) Dahmer was initially more precise and careful when it came to disposing of bodies than your average serial killer. He had an aptitude for science - something which obviously helped in his grisly stock-in-trade. As his grasp on reality (never very firm to begin with) started to frazzle and evaporate, Dahmer would become less studious at removing traces of his crimes.

(153) During his police confession, Jeffrey Dahmer was asked if he ate human body parts plain. He replied that he ate them with salt & pepper and steak sauce.

(154) Dahmer used formaldehyde to preserve body parts.

(155) Necrophilia dates back hundreds of years and has been documented in Greek mythology.

(156) Dahmer claimed he felt brief remorse for the victim but this did not last. Mostly, he felt excited.

(157) When he was captured, Jeffrey Dahmer told the police that he retained the skulls and bones of his victims because he wanted to use them to construct a place of meditation.

(158) Dahmer initially plead not guilty when he was charged. He then decided to plead guilty by reason of insanity.

(159) There was criticism of the jury selection for Dahmer's trial because most of his victims were black and yet the jury was almost completely white.

(160) Dahmer was surrounded by bullet proof glass during his trial. Given the anger he'd aroused in the local community there was a genuine fear that someone might try to kill him.

(161) Dahmer's defence team at the trial went into great detail describing his grisly crimes because they believed this was the only way to convince the jury that he was insane. No sane person, they argued, could have done the things that Dahmer did. The prosecution argued though that Dahmer knew exactly what he was doing and wasn't insane at all.

(162) Dahmer was sentenced to fifteen consecutive life terms, a total of 957 years in prison.

(163) It took a jury only five hours to find Dahmer guilty.

(164) Jeffrey Dahmer's brother David did not show up at the trial. David was greatly affected by the shocking revelations and wanted nothing to do with the media or his brother.

(165) Jeffrey Dahmer's brother David later changed his name when his brother was revealed to be a serial killer and cannibal.

(166) Serial killers who are captured often fall into two categories. Those who (ludicrously) insist they are innocent and those who seem to enjoy openly talking about crimes. Dahmer was the latter.

(167) The police found some incense sticks in Jeffrey Dahmer's apartment. He is believed to have purchased these to put in his macabre meditation shrine composed of victim skulls and bones.
(168) The police found two bags in Jeffrey Dahmer's fridge that contained human hearts.

(169) Jeffrey Dahmer had several gay porn VHS tapes in his apartment when it was searched.

(170) The polaroids Damer took of his victims included ones he took during actual acts of necrophilia.

(171) Dahmer had some plant pots in his apartment when he was captured. He liked plants and gardening.

(172) A local real estate magnate named Joseph Zilber raised money to buy Dahmer's fridge, tools, and belongings after his trial so that they could be destroyed. The community didn't want anyone to use Dahmer's artifacts and affects as part of some macabre display or money making scheme.

(173) Dahmer's youngest victim was fourteen years old.

(174) Dahmer was ruled to be sane and not suffering from a mental disorder at the time of each of the 15 murders for which he was tried

(175) The police found ether in Jeffrey Dahmer's apartment. This is an illicit drug to induce sedation. Dahmer said ether didn't work very well so he used sleeping pills instead.

(176) Dahmer had chloroform in his apartment when he was captured.

(177) Dahmer said he purchased his handcuffs from an army surplus store.

(178) Most experts think the theory that serial killers are 'bad seeds' who were born bad is a myth. You can't be born bad. Environments and experiences turn people twisted and bad - not genetics.

(179) A lot of serial killers seem to have had incidents of indecent exposure at a young age. Randall Woodfield, Ted Bundy, and Jeffrey Dahmer are examples.

(180) The FBI once stated that, according to their research, around 70% of serial killers have experienced drug or alcohol addictions in their life.

(181) Dahmer served his time at the Columbia Correctional Institution in Portage, Wisconsin.

(182) Dahmer was tried in Milwaukee for 15 counts of first-degree murder. The death penalty was not an option in the state.

(183) Dahmer did some interviews while in prison. Despite the gruesome and unfathomable nature of his crimes, Dahmer seemed alarmingly normal and mundane in interviews. He was articulate and soft-spoken.

(184) Believe it or not there is a comedy horror film called Dahmer vs. Gacy where these two killers are cloned, get loose, and do battle. Though played for laughs, Dahmer vs. Gacy is strictly bottom of the barrel amateur hour and best avoided.

(185) Jeffrey Dahmer had a vintage fish tank in his apartment.

(186) Jeffrey Dahmer's apartment building was demolished after his capture. No one wanted to live there anymore.

(187) When he was in prison, Dahmer, for a joke, put up a sign in his cell which read "Cannibals anonymous meeting tonight."

(188) Dahmer was baptized while in prison.

(189) When the police searched Jeffrey Dahmer's apartment he had VHS tapes of Return of the Jedi, The Exorcist III, Chippendales Tall Dark and Handsome, and an episode of The Cosby Show.

(190) Jeffrey Dahmer said that he never really understood why he did the awful things he did. He said it was like some dark compulsion he couldn't control.

(191) Dennis Nilsen is to this day sometimes dubbed Britain's Jeffrey Dahmer - although Dahmer actually came after Nilsen. You might suggest that Dahmer WAS actually the American Dennis Nilsen - though with some qualifications. The story of Jeffrey Dahmer was, in some areas, even more grisly than the story of Dennis Nilsen. One would hardly think that was possible. What could be worse than Dennis Nilsen?

(192) It is uncanny to note the similarities between Dahmer and Nilsen. Both of them were in the army. Both of them were big drinkers. Both of them picked their victims up in bars. Both of them were highly intelligent. Both of them were gay. Both of them wore aviator glasses. And both were motivated by necrophilia. Nilsen and Dahmer both said exactly the same thing when they were captured. Dahmer and Nilsen were both terrified of being alone. They said they enjoyed the company of dead people because it was better than nothing.

(193) At his trial, Jeffrey Dahmer said that the only thing he desired was death.

(194) Between 30% to 40% of serial killers display abnormal brainwave patterns.

(195) John Backderf, who knew Jeffrey Dahmer at school, wrote a comic called My Friend Dahmer - which was later turned into a film. Backderf said there was always a darkness about Dahmer and he wasn't the sort of person you'd want to be alone with.

(196) Jeffrey Dahmer had a very (what else?) deadpan sense of humour. He would tell journalists that human biceps tasted like a good cut of steak.

(197) The literal translation of necrophilia is 'love of the dead'. Necrophilia is a pathological fascination with dead bodies which takes the form of a desire to engage with them in sexual activities.

(198) Necrophilia is a common postmortem activity for sexual serial killers because it doesn't give the victim the opportunity reject the offender.

(199) Necrophilia was first documented in Krafft-Ebing's Psychopathia Sexualis.

(200) Dahmer's favourite movie was The Exorcist III.

(201) It was the possessed Gemini killer in The Exorcist III which fascinated Dahmer the most. The Exorcist III is a very underrated sequel which has become something of a cult film over the years. It has a terrific central performance by George C. Scott.

(202) Dahmer ate the livers of some of his victims.

(203) John Backderf said that when he heard that a former classmate of his was a serial killer cannibal, Dahmer was only the second person he thought of. Backderf had initially presumed it might be someone else he used to know at the school!

(204) John Backderf said he decided to skip Dahmer's trial because he simply couldn't face going and listening to all that grim evidence.

(205) When he was at school, Dahmer would amuse his friends by pretending to have a seizure. This joke was known as 'doing a Dahmer'.

(206) Dahmer said that when he worked in the chocolate factory he once took a victim's head to work with him and kept it in his locker.

(207) Dahmer said that when he killed someone he got himself into a mindset where the victim was not a person but an object designed purely for his own pleasure.

(208) Jeffrey Dahmer worked at the chocolate factory for about six years before he was fired.

(209) There was a long gap of nearly ten years between Dahmer's first and second murders. This is somewhat uncommon for serial killers.

(210) Dahmer said his first murder was not planned.

(211) Serial killers, as a group, don't really conform to any one type. Some are quite smart and some are dumb. Some of them are organised and some are disorganised. Some are loners and some have families. Ultimately they are just like us and an eclectic mix.

(212) Dahmer said he tried to get into Satanism and the occult when he was a teenager. He maintained an interest in such things throughout his life.

(213) Dahmer would apparently tease prison guards by telling them that he liked to bite people.

(214) In the wake of the Dahmer case there were understandable criticisms of the police on the issue of race. Some contended (whether fairly or unfairly) that because Dahmer's victims were mostly African-American and gay they were more invisible and 'forgotten' in society and the police displayed little interest in investigating their deaths. This was somewhat similar to the Dennis Nilsen case. Nilsen's victims were mostly gay and some in the gay community in London felt the police were indifferent to gay men going missing because of institutional homophobia.

(215) The police found some acne cream in Dahmer's apartment when he was arrested.

(216) Dahmer was a fan of heavy metal music.

(217) Dahmer would visit Chicago as a young man. He liked to

go to gay strip clubs.

(218) The police questioned Dahmer about many unsolved murders when he was arrested but they could never connect him to any of them. Dahmer, not unreasonably, told the police that he'd confessed to being a cannibal necrophile so why would he tried and hide his involvement with other murders?

(219) When he first went to prison, Dahmer was placed in protective custody for his own safety.

(220) Dahmer grew tired of isolation in prison and persuaded the prison authorities to let him eat and mix with other prisoners. This ultimately led to his death.

(221) Dahmer didn't serve much of his sentence in the end. In 1994, another prisoner (a convicted murderer named Christopher Scarver) attacked Dahmer and another inmate named Jesse Anderson with an iron bar. The attack was so violent that Dahmer later died in hospital. He was 34 years-old and the life of one of the most infamous serial killers in American history had ended.

(222) Christopher Scarver, who murdered Dahmer in prison, claimed (rather dubiously) that Dahmer infuriated other inmates by manipulating his food into the shape of human body parts.

(223) Dahmer had already been attacked even before his prison death. A previous incident occurred where a prisoner tried to slash his throat.

(224) Osvaldo Durruthy was the first person to try and kill Dahmer in prison. Durruthy said this failed because the 'razor shank' he constructed wasn't strong enough. Durruthy said he punched Dahmer in the head several times before the prison guards arrived.

(225) It is rather ironic that Dahmer was killed in the same

fashion that he killed his first victim - bludgeoned by a heavy gym object.

(226) Those who suspect that Dahmer killed Adam Walsh think that one of the reasons he denied involvement in this murder because he was ashamed of the fact that he killed a child. This is only a theory though. There is no concrete evidence that Dahmer committed this murder.

(227) Dahmer had four books about tropical fish in his apartment when he was arrested.

(228) Dahmer said he decided to quit Florida when he woke up on the beach one morning and saw there was a rat sitting on his stomach.

(229) Dahmer would cut a hole in the stomach of his victims and use it as a way to have sexual intercourse.

(230) Preston Davis was one of the men who claimed Dahmer sexually assaulted him in the army. David said that Dahmer drugged and raped him while they were on field exercises in Belgium.

(231) Preston Davis (who is black) said that Dahmer was a racist who became horrible when he was drunk. The claims of Preston Davis contradict the general assumption that the race of Dahmer's victims had nothing to do with why they were chosen.

(232) Preston Davis said he blocked out the incident with Dahmer for many years because it was too distressing for him to cope with.

(233) The police found a total of 74 polaroid photographs depicting dead victims in Dahmer's apartment.

(234) When he was in custody, Dahmer said that if he'd had a video camera he would have shot film of his dead victims.

(235) Billy Capshaw was the other soldier who alleged that Dahmer abused him. "It was Dr Jekyll and Mr Hyde," Capshaw said. "I was in a room I was scared to come out of. I would steal Jeff's money thinking that if he didn't have any money, that he wouldn't drink anymore and therefore wouldn't hurt me anymore. He beat me so badly for that, and to stop me from screaming, he hit me harder. I thought about killing him, and I thought about killing myself."

(236) Billy Capshaw said he complained about Dahmer but the army didn't take his claims seriously and took no action.

(237) The album on Dahmer's record player when he was arrested was Buried Dreams by Clock DVA.

(238) Studies have shown that 74% of serial killers murder their victims within a circumscribed geographic area. They tend to have a comfort zone. That comfort zone is a specific local area which they know very well. Serial killers often seem to be creatures of habit. They feel more comfortable killing in an area that they have some knowledge of and are familiar with.

(239) Jeffrey Dahmer suffered from hay fever.

(240) The police officers John A. Balcerzak and Joseph P. Gabrish have both defended their actions in various interviews. They said that Dahmer seemed perfectly calm and normal to them and they had no idea that Konerak Sinthasomphone was so young. Dahmer told the police officers that Sinthasomphone was nineteen. John A. Balcerzak and Joseph P. Gabrish said they had little information to go on that night and genuinely believed that this was just a case of someone having too much to drink.

(241) John A. Balcerzak remained a police officer until his retirement in 2017.

(242) Most of the very famous serial killers eschew guns

because firearms destroy the intimacy of murder.

(243) The police officers who arrested Dahmer realised he was a serial killer when they found the polaroids of his victims in the bedroom. Dahmer had been trying to get to the bedroom first to hide these pictures and his haste in suddenly moving towards the bedroom made the officers suspicious.

(244) The fire department had to be called to take away the big chemical filled blue drum Dahmer had in his apartment when he was arrested.

(245) Dahmer had a human scalp in one of his drawers when he was arrested.

(246) Thankfully, the chances of you walking past a serial killer in the street or encountering one in real life are slim to say the least. There really aren't that many of them compared to the general population. Scientific American said that serial killers only account for 1% of the yearly murders in America.

(247) As a kid, Dahmer was briefly in the Boy Scouts and went camping with them. Dahmer said he didn't enjoy this much.

(248) The woman who had the apartment above Jeffrey Dahmer DID complain about the smell and got moved. Those in charge of the building presumed it must be a sewage problem.

(249) Nothing has been done with the site where Dahmer's old apartment building used to be. Many suggested the site should become a memorial garden or a children's play area.

(250) Dahmer's neighbours complained to the police more than once about strange noises and smells coming from Dahmer's apartment. The police simply ignored these calls though and did not investigate Dahmer.

(251) Dahmer dissected three men at his grandmother's house.

She obviously had no idea what her grandson was doing in the basement.

(252) The only member of his family that Jeffrey Dahmer kept in very regular touch with before his capture was his grandmother.

(253) Dahmer's grandmother was a retired teacher.

(254) One of Dahmer's colleagues at the chocolate factory said Dahmer was always falling asleep at work. This is doubtless part of the reason why he got fired.

(255) Rudy Bayron, who worked with Dahmer at the chocolate factory, said that Dahmer would bring peanut butter and honey sandwiches to work and cut them with a twelve inch knife. Dahmer used to joke to colleagues that he used the knife to kill people.

(256) The FBI once estimated that serial killers are responsible for about 170 murders a year in America. As there are thousands of murders a year in America, serial killers account for a very small number of victims.

(257) It is estimated that 15% of serial killer victims were chosen at random and just happened (unfortunately for them) to be in the wrong place at the wrong time.

(258) Dahmer was an outcast from an early age - although he was always quite intelligent.

(259) The FBI say that serial killers tend to be cautious with their first murder. They will typically choose a vulnerable person who is somewhat disconnected from conventional 9-5 society - like a homeless person, sex worker, or hitch-hiking drifter.

(260) In a story so bizarre it sounds completely made up, after his death there was a battle for custody of Jeffrey Dahmer's brain between his parents. Dahmer's mother wanted his brain

to be donated to science because this was what Jeffrey Dahmer had apparently requested. Dahmer's father didn't want this to happen though. In the end Dahmer's father got his way and Jeffrey Dahmer's brain was cremated along with the rest of him.

(261) A Jeffrey Dahmer signed Valentines Day card on collectible sites can go for $5000.

(262) Studies have indicated that serial killers do not have natural human emotions like fear, happiness, and anxiety. As a consequence, serial killers need to do something extreme to experience any feelings at all.

(263) Dahmer always seemed to have a morbid fascination with the science of death and decomposition.

(264) Dahmer purchased contact lenses with yellow tint. It is said that he did this in tribute to the yellow eyed emperor in the original Star Wars movies.

(265) Serial killers do not have a rational and logical voice in their head telling them that a course of action is wrong. They will ignore and banish any such thoughts. They have no empathy, compassion, or remorse for their victims.

(266) Jeffrey Dahmer's father Lionel Dahmer once wrote a book called A Father's Story in which he tried (as far as anyone possibly could) to understand how his son had become one of the most infamous figures in criminal history.

(267) It is estimated that around 7% of serial killers in America served in the military.

(268) When he was in custody, Dahmer said he would do anything possible to get the death penalty. Most believe he wasn't sincere about this.

(269) It has been estimated in some studies that only around

22% of serial killers use firearms when they kill.

(270) Cruelty to animals is usually regarded to be a warning sign that someone might be capable of being a serial killer. Dahmer displayed no such warnings though. He loved animals and was kind to them.

(271) Dahmer didn't have a car and so had to rely on buses and cabs to get around.

(272) Dahmer's colleagues at the chocolate factory expressed surprise in the media when Dahmer's crimes came to light. They'd considered Jeffrey Dahmer to be meek and not in the least bit scary. He didn't seem like a killer at all to them. This is quite common when it comes to serial killers. Ted Bundy's friends and family initially refused to believe he was a serial killer when he was captured for the last time. When the horrors of Cromwell Street were revealed, the neigbours of Fred and Rose West expressed amazement that these two seemingly placid and friendly people could be capable of murder.

(273) As part of his probation for previous sexual convictions, a probation officer was supposed to visit Dahmer each week to check up on him. However, this never happened because the probation officer in question was too busy with other cases. Had the probation visits gone ahead then Dahmer's murderous activities would have been rumbled much sooner. To be fair to the probation service in question, they obviously could have had no way of knowing that Dahmer was a serial killer cannibal.

(274) Dahmer's high school guidance counsellor said that Dahmer was impossible to get to know or figure out because he very rarely said anything at all.

(275) The police detectives who questioned Dahmer after his arrest said he was shy to the point where it took a couple of days before he was comfortable making eye contact with them.

(276) After he was arrested and the case was first reported in the media, Dahmer's apartment building was besieged with camera crews and media from around the world and members of the public who had just come to have a gawp at the place where this infamous cannibal had lived.

(277) Dental records were used to identify the skulls found in Dahmer's apartment.

(278) A study once found that 86% of serial killers had violent sexual fantasies that involved mutilation and restrained victims.

(279) The gay community didn't like the way that Dahmer's sexuality was sometimes a morbid focus in reporting of his crimes. They rightly argued that Dahmer was no more representative of gay people than Ted Bundy was of straight people.

(280) Bridget Geiger Jeffrey Dahmer's friends arranged for Dahmer to take her to the prom.

(281) Dahmer's parents got divorced in 1978. Dahmer's brother David went to live with his mother while Jeffrey Dahmer lived with his father and stepmother Shari. Dahmer would also obviously spend some time living with his grandmother.

(282) Dahmer's high school yearbook states that he had some participation in the school newspaper.

(283) Dahmer's school grade point average was 2.0 on a four point scale.

(284) A man who knew Dahmer at the chocolate factory said Dahmer hated working there. He also said Dahmer was quite conservative in his political views and used to complain about the welfare system supporting people who were too lazy to work.

(285) Dahmer was trained how to use hand grenades when he was in the army.

(286) Dahmer worried his family at a young age because he was withdrawn and had no hobbies. He didn't do the normal things that other boys did.

(287) Dahmer's stepmother said he was always a loner and impossible to get to know.

(288) A collector once put Dahmer's prison glasses up for sale. He wanted $150,000 for them.

(289) Dahmer's traffic violation came while he had the remains of his first victim in the trunk. If the police officers had searched the car then Dahmer's killing career would have been over almost as soon as it started.

(290) Dahmer had three room mates at college. They all thought he was weird.

(291) Jeffrey Dahmer's crime spree lasted for thirteen years. There were thirteen letters in his name and his apartment number contained the number 13 too.

(292) When he was in prison and pondering on how badly his life turned out, Dahmer said he should have finished college and gone into real estate or sales. He wished he could have just been a normal person.

(293) Dahmer said that after his first murder he tried to 'bury' this experience and forget about it. That proved to be impossible though.

(294) Dahmer had a bolt lock on the outside of his bedroom door. This was obviously designed to lock people in.

(295) Dahmer was overweight when he quit college. When he joined the army he was put on a strict diet to get into shape.

(296) Some of Dahmer's army colleagues said that he bragged about killing someone before he joined the military. They just presumed he was joking or making it up.

(297) When he lived in Florida, Dahmer worked for a time at a sandwich shop called Sunshine Subs. The owner took pity on Dahmer and gave him a job after he caught Dahmer looking for food in the dumpster.

(298) After he killed his first victim, Dahmer sliced open the stomach because he was curious to see what the insides of a human looked like.

(299) Dahmer had a book about numerology in his apartment when he was captured. Numerology is an ancient study that draws meaning from different numbers.

(300) When he worked as a phlebotomist, Dahmer stole a vial of blood and tried to drink it. He didn't like the taste though.

(301) When he worked in the sandwich shop in Miami, Dahmer once found a dead body out the back of the shop. This was a rare case of a dead body in Dahmer's life that he had nothing to do with!

(302) Ken Haupert, who owned Sunshine Subs, said Dahmer was his own worst enemy and often turned up to work drunk.

(303) One of the main reasons why people suspect Dahmer of having killed Adam Walsh in Florida is that eyewitnesses said the child was abducted in a blue van. Sunshine Subs, where Dahmer worked at the time, had a blue van that employees used.

(304) There is a theory (purely a theory) that if Dahmer killed Adam Walsh he kept quiet about this because he knew Florida had the death penalty. This theory obviously proposes that Dahmer's bluster about wanting to die was merely that - bluster. In reality he was fearful of execution.

(305) Another factor in why some still contend that Dahmer killed Adam Walsh is that the police artist impression of the eyewitness suspect looked alarmingly like Jeffrey Dahmer.

(306) There was a brief moment in time during his school years where Dahmer had friends and was regarded to be quite funny. This didn't last very long.

(307) The cab driver who Dahmer hired to transport the big barrel (which he used to dissolve bodies) to his apartment later said he was tempted to ask Dahmer what he was going to use the barrel for but decided not to be 'nosey'.

(308) When he was revealed to be a serial killer, the police in Germany (where Dahmer, as we have noted, served in the U.S Army) had to investigate possible links between Dahmer and unsolved murders in their country. They were not able to come up with any evidence though which suggested Dahmer might have killed anyone in Germany.

(309) When he was in the army, Dahmer's colleagues took him to a brothel once. Dahmer, who had no interest in women, managed to sneak out and flee.

(310) When he worked at Sunshine Subs, Dahmer became friends with an English girl who worked there. She was in the United States illegally and asked Dahmer to marry her so she could get the legal right to stay in America. As you might suspect, Dahmer declined to go along with this plan.

(311) Dahmer was a heavy smoker. This was a habit he picked up in the army.

(312) Dahmer said he felt a great sense of loss whenever he had to dispose of some human remains in the garbage. He wished he could keep all parts of his victims.

(313) Dahmer said he nearly always drunk when his murders took place.

(314) Jeffrey Dahmer told the police that he wasn't an alcoholic and was perfectly capable of going days at a time without a drink.

(315) Dahmer told the police that he only ate people he liked.

(316) When he lived with his grandmother, Dahmer was questioned by her about the foul smells coming from the basement. Dahmer told his grandmother that the smell was coming from the cat litter tray down there.

(317) Dahmer had some creative excuses for the smells that came from his apartment. When he was questioned by the building supervisor about strange smells Dahmer told him that the smell came from changing the water in his fish tank.

(318) Dahmer said that when you remove the skin from a head it looks rather like a mask you can wear.

(319) Dahmer said he tried to preserve the face of one victim but he was unable to do this because the chemical solution he used destroyed it.

(320) Jeffrey Dahmer targeted victims with smooth skin. He didn't like body hair.

(321) Dahmer said he always knew before he went out if he was going to kill someone that night.

(322) Dahmer would prepare the spiked drink for victims before he went out and leave it in his kitchen.

(323) When the Dahmer case came to light there was a certain amount of media coverage about the alleged link between horror movies and killers like Dahmer. This felt rather overblown and tenuous. Many of us love horror movies and yet have never harmed so much as a fly. Dahmer was destined for trouble with or without horror films.

(324) Dahmer told the police that before he was captured he had planned to dispose of all the evidence (body parts and bones) and then go to a homeless shelter until he could find himself another job and apartment. Dahmer conceded to the police though that even if he'd managed to do all of this he most likely would have started killing again and thus the vicious cycle would begin afresh somewhere else.

(325) Dahmer only targeted victims who were in their teens or twenties. Anyone above that age didn't interest him.

(326) Bridget Geiger, rather self-deprecatingly, said she ended up going to the prom with Dahmer because she wasn't very popular. She had no other offers.

(327) Dahmer's mother Joyce passed away from cancer in 2000.

(328) Jeffrey Dahmer didn't wear his trademark aviator glasses at the trial. There was a reason for this. Dahmer got nervous with eye contact and crowds so his defence team felt that if all around him seemed fuzzy and out of focus he would be calmer.

(329) You can actually go on a walking tour in Milwaukee where you visit Dahmer's old haunts. It's a lot like one of those Jack the Ripper tours in London.

(330) Dahmer put Crisco on a human bicep he ate. Crisco is a brand of vegetable oil.

(331) Dahmer's work colleagues at the chocolate factory said he was always broke. After paying his rent and trawling around the town buying booze and looking for victims, Dahmer never had much money left.

(332) Dahmer chose his apartment because it was cheap and close to where he worked.

(333) Milwaukee County District Attorney E. Michael McCann argued at the trial that Dahmer had passed up opportunities to kill certain people because he judged that the risk of being caught was too great. the legal subtext of this was pretty obvious. McCann was saying that Dahmer was shrewd and calculating and knew exactly what he was doing. He wasn't insane at all.

(334) Dahmer's apartment only had one bedroom.

(335) Dahmer's defence team were annoyed when he changed his plea to guilty by reasons of insanity. One would have thought though that proving Dahmer was insane would have been more feasible than proving he didn't commit those murders!

(336) The gun that Dahmer briefly owned was a Magnum. His father told him to get rid of this gun.

(337) Monster: The Jeffrey Dahmer Story, a 2022 Netflix series starring Evan Peters as Dahmer, became the most watched show in Netflix history.

(338) Surviving relatives of the victims of Dahmer were rather dismayed by the release of Monster: The Jeffrey Dahmer Story. There is an ongoing debate about whether or not the media and entertainment world should be making 'celebrities' of the likes of Dahmer and Ted Bundy.

(339) A 1993 film called The Secret Life: Jeffrey Dahmer starred Carl Crew as Dahmer. This film is rather unique because Dahmer was still alive when it came out.

(340) A relative of Dahmer victim Errol Lindsey lunged at Dahmer in court had to be carried away by bailiffs. Emotions were running high - for understandable and tragic reasons.

(341) How did Dahmer steal the mannequin from a store? Dahmer said he hid and got himself locked in and when

everyone went home and they closed up he put a sleeping bag over it and took a taxi home.

(342) Dahmer said he kept the mannequin for about two weeks. He said he pretended it was a real person and cuddled it in bed.

(343) Dahmer said that, when dissecting a body, separating the arm and leg joints is one of the most difficult tasks.

(344) Dahmer's lawyer later said that Jeffrey Dahmer was the 'wimpiest' and most placid person he'd ever met. That merely made Dahmer's crimes even more chilling. He was a wolf in sheep's clothing - to use a cliche.

(345) The judge at Dahmer's trial later said that presiding over this case had been a very disturbing and difficult experience.

(346) Dahmer's murders escalated in the end to the point where they almost piled up on one another. One could argue that he began as an organised serial killer but as his descent into madness and depravity went on he became a disorganised serial killer.

(347) The Milwaukee Police Department implemented some reforms in the wake of the Dahmer case. Their key concerns were that they had patently failed to notice a number of local black men had gone missing and were also plainly distrusted by the gay community. As far as the police (and public) were concerned there was plenty of room for improvement in community relations and attitudes to minorities. Dahmer, tragically, had shone a light on these failings.

(348) Jeffrey Dahmer said all his teenage friends were straight and he never knew any gay people when he was growing-up.

(349) Dahmer got a lot of mail in prison. Some people even sent him money. In 1994 a newspaper reported that Dahmer had been sent about $12,000 through these 'penpals'.

(350) Jeffrey Dahmer received marriage proposals from women while in prison. The term for this strange phenemenon is hybristophilia. Hybristophilia is sometimes referred to as Bonnie and Clyde syndrome. 'Hybristophiliacs,' wrote Owlcation, 'are people who are sexually aroused and attracted to people who have committed cruel, gruesome crimes such as murder and rape. It occurs more often in women than in men. There are two categories of hybristophiliacs: The first is Passive Hybristophilia. Every year, notorious criminals receive romantic and sexual fan mail from admirers. These letter-writing groupies (known as SKGs -- serial killer groupies) have no desire in taking part of criminal activity, yet are attracted to men behind bars.'

(351) The relatives of Dahmer's victims were awarded $80 million compensation in a civil suit. Dahmer obviously had no way of paying this sort of money so the relatives simply got a share of the money from the sale of Dahmer's stuff.

(352) One person even sent Dahmer a typewriter while he was in prison. Dahmer would use it to reply to letters.

(353) When he was in prison Dahmer got 'fan mail' from as far away as Europe and South Africa.

(354) It seems that hybristophilia clouds any sense of logic or taste. Women (and sometimes men) are fascinated by serial killers and even become overwhelmed by the desire to meet them and look after them. They rationalise this conduct by refusing to believe the killer is guilty or simply tell themselves they are doing a kind deed to someone who is lonely and an outcast in society. No matter how awful the killer is, you can guarantee that killer has received fan mail and that there are probably women out there who would be perfectly willing to meet them and, in some cases, even marry them.

(355) You used to be able to buy the 'Jeffrey Dahmer victim doll', which was 'fully dismemberable' and '100% cannibal approved.' This toy would have set you back $295. When it

comes to true crime memorabilia, you can buy literally anything. There is naturally a debate about the morality of this sort of business. Relatives of victims have raised a lot of concern. It would obviously be distressing to see some killer who had murdered one of your relatives turned into a bobblehead toy or trading card or grinning in some prison photograph on sale. However, those who sell these items feel it is relatively harmless and liken it to those who have an interest in the occult or horror. People are naturally interested in dark things.

(356) When he was in prison, Dahmer was deluged with letters from a woman who was obsessed with him. She would send him a letter a day. Literally all she did was write endless letters to Dahmer. It was obviously a bit much for Dahmer though and he simply stopped replying in the hope that she would stop writing.

(357) Believe it or not, the majority of serial killers are usually deemed to be sane when subjected to tests.

(358) Dahmer said he would cut the noses off victims before he boiled the heads.

(359) Dahmer and Dennis Nilsen were similar in their disposal of remains. Both boiled heads and both flushed flesh down the toilet. They both ended up with cupboards and drawers full of body parts.

(360) You can find YouTube footage of Dahmer's father visiting his son in prison. Jeffery Dahmer comes across as very reserved and polite in the footage. He was not a man who showed any emotion.

(361) The frustrating thing for Lionel Dahmer is that he knew his son was intelligent enough to get a good education and a good job but Jeffery Dahmer simply lacked the ability to apply himself to anything.

(362) Despite the uncanny similarities between them (aside from cannibalism), Jeffrey Dahmer was unaware of the Dennis Nilsen case.

(363) Dahmer was known as 'Jeff' to his friends and family.

(364) Dahmer drank a lot of coffee.

(365) Dahmer was fascinated by roadkill growing up.

(366) The trial of Dahmer became a bit of a media circus in the end. The media and public were fascinated by this mild mannered ordinary looking man they'd heard all these harrowing and gruesome things about.

(367) Most of the residents of Dahmer's apartment building were black or Latino. As one might expect of a serial killer cannibal with (quite literally) skeletons in the closet, Dahmer kept himself to himself and didn't interact with them much.

(368) Dahmer managed to get prescriptions for sleeping pills quite easily because he said that as a nightshift worker he needed them to sleep during the day.

(369) A set of cutlery belonging to Jeffrey Dahmer sold for $300 per item in 2022.

(370) Those who remembered Dahmer from Club 219 say he would sit on his own drinking and rarely talk to anyone.

(371) Dahmer was arrested for Disorderly conduct in 1985 for threatening to shoot a barmaid for not giving him a drink.

(372) The man Dahmer killed in the hotel was 25 year-old Steven Tuomi. Dahmer said he woke up with bruised knuckles and realised he'd battered Steven to death. Dahmer believes that because he'd drunk a large amount of rum the previous evening he had some sort of blackout which made him forget everything that had happened.

(373) Dahmer said he had pounded Steven Tuomi so hard that Steven's ribs were broken. As usual, Dahmer had drugged the victim first so there would be no resistance.

(374) Wisconsin abolished the death penalty in 1853. Dahmer would almost certainly have been sentenced to death had his crimes taken place in a state like Florida or Texas. Not that this would have happened quickly though. Prisoners can be on 'death row' for decades.

(375) Christopher Scarver, the man who killed Dahmer in prison, suggested to the media that the prison guards left him alone with Dahmer on purpose because they wanted Dahmer dead.

(376) Christopher Scarver was already serving life for murder so he probably figured he didn't have much to lose by killing Dahmer. Scarver said that God told him to kill Dahmer.

(377) After disposing of the body, Dahmer kept Steven Tuomi's head for two weeks. He stored it in his closet.

(378) John A. Balcerzak later served as president of the Milwaukee Police Association (the police union) from 2005 to 2009.

(379) Dahmer had to borrow some clothes from a detective for a court appearance so the detective gave Dahmer one of his son's shirts. When the detective gave the shirt back to his son the kid threw the shirt away because of its association with Dahmer. That was clearly a mistake as that shirt would be worth a fortune on murderabilia sites today!

(380) Dahmer's mother tried to commit suicide in the wake of the case by leaving her oven on. She was found unconscious but survived.

(381) Because they don't have normal human emotions or feelings, serial killers tend to see their victims as mere objects

to do with as they please. The fact that they are causing pain, suffering, and death doesn't bother serial killers. They don't worry about things like this.

(382) Christopher Scarver, the man who killed Dahmer, is obviously still behind bars. He writes poetry and has put some of these 'collections' on Amazon. He has occasionally threatened to write a book about killing Jeffrey Dahmer.

(383) It would probably be fair to say that the relatives of Dahmer's victims didn't shed too many tears when they learned he'd been beaten to death in prison. Some though did tell the media they would have preferred Dahmer to endure life in prison as that would probably have been worse than death.

(384) There were instances of Dahmer sedating someone but not killing them. It is quite rare for serial killers to let a potential victim go like this. It is generally assumed that Dahmer did not kill these people because he deemed those specific situations too risky.

(385) No one at the chocolate factory initially knew Dahmer was gay because he never talked about his private life.

(386) Dahmer flunked Anthropology, Classical Civilizations, and Administrative Science when he was (briefly) at college.

(387) When he dissected a victim, Dahmer suspended the torso above his bath to drain away the blood.

(388) Dahmer was extradited to Ohio to be tried for the murder of his first victim Steven Hicks. He pled guilty and had another life sentence added to his slate.

(389) Dahmer seemed to be articulate in prison interviews that his lack of belief in God was a factor in his murders. He felt that in a Godless universe there was no one to punish him for his crimes. Dahmer, like so many killers and criminals,

only became religious after he was captured.

(390) Christopher Scarver claimed that his murder of Dahmer was not premeditated. This is contradicted though by the fact that he'd smuggled an iron bar to his fateful work detail with Dahmer.

(391) The mother of Dahmer victim Steven Hicks filed a $50 million a wrongful death suit against Jeffrey Dahmer's parents. The legal action alleged that Dahmer's parents were negligent and knew their son was deviant and dangerous. The suit never had much chance of success and Dahmer's parents obviously didn't have $50 million anyway.

(392) Twelve of Dahmer's victims were killed in his apartment.

(393) Dahmer killed two people at his parent's home and three at his grandmother's house.

(394) Radford University's 2016 report found that 1987 was the most prolific year ever for serial killers in the United States. Serial killers were responsible for 389 deaths that year. 1987 was a fairly quiet year for Dahmer though as he only killed one person.

(395) Most serial killers are in their twenties or thirties. A large number of serial killers kill for the first time in their teens or twenties.

(396) Serial killers today are at a low level compared to the 1970s, 80s, and even 90s. There are a number of factors for why this is the case. The fact that most nations have extensive CCTV camera systems in cities and towns now is one obvious reason why it's harder to be a serial killer today. We also have cell phones and GPS.

Another important change from the serial killer festooned seventies and eighties is that many sex workers today operate online rather than walk the streets. They are able to 'vet' the people they meet more than was possible in the past. Now, this doesn't make them 100% safe but sex workers (so often the victims of famous serial killers) are a lot safer today than they used to be.

Another theory for why there aren't as many serial killers is that the police have more technology at their disposal now and are simply better at catching murderers than they used to be. Forensics and DNA profiling is much more advanced today than it was in the 1970s or 1980s. The police today can convict someone from a single strand of hair found at a crime scene. This sort of forensic technology means that serial killers today have no margin of error at all anymore. One other obvious theory as to why serial killer murders are not as common as they used to be is that modern society is less risk adverse than it was in the 1970s and 1980s. People and (especially) teenagers and children are more clued up about danger. Society, for better or worse, is less innocent than it used to be. People go out less than they used.

(397) The overwhelming majority of serial killers (over 80%) are white.

(398) A study by Radford University suggested that 46% of serial killers killed simply for the enjoyment.

(399) The police had to trash Dahmer's apartment to rule out the possibility that he'd hidden body parts in the walls.

(400) Dahmer, you probably won't be surprised to hear, showed no emotion when he was found guilty at his trial. This was in stark contrast to relatives of the victims. They clapped and cheered when they heard the verdict.

(401) Dahmer was fired from his job as a phlebotomist after about ten months. His duties involved dealing with blood samples. It is said that Dahmer didn't like this job much because the pay wasn't very good.

(402) Colleagues at the chocolate factory said that Dahmer wasn't very chatty at all (to put it mildly) and spent his lunch break reading books about tropical fish.

(403) In terms of the number of victims, Dahmer is about the fourteenth most prolific serial killer in American history.

(404) Dahmer was beaten up by colleagues in the army once after his infractions earned the platoon disciplinary penalties.

(405) When his trial began, Dahmer was taken to the courtroom handcuffed to a wheelchair. He was then released and allowed to walk in and take his seat.

(406) Dahmer would usually offer his victims $50 to come back to his apartment for a photography session.

(407) Dahmer performed his 'zombification' experiments on four of the victims.

(408) Dahmer said that after he killed someone he would lay next to the body and pretend that person was still alive.

(409) Tracy Edwards, who sealed Dahmer's fate when he escaped from the apartment, said that Dahmer was very friendly and normal at first but then something seemed to 'snap' and he became a completely different person - someone terrifying.

(410) Dahmer barely said anything to his legal team throughout the trial. He simply sat still and emotionless. He only spoke to his legal team if one of them asked him a question. His answers were short and brief.
(411) When he was in prison, Dahmer said he missed his fish and aquarium. That had been just about his only sane healthy hobby.

(412) Dahmer used the internal organs of his victims for sexual gratification.

(413) After Dahmer's apartment building was demolished, ghoulish souvenir hunters started to take away bricks and even dirt. The vacant lot had to be fenced off to deter this.

(414) Dahmer said he took photographs of his victims when they were still 'fresh' so that he could remember what they looked like.

(415) When he dissected his victims and boiled the heads, Dahmer used a spoon to scoop out brain matter.

(416) Dahmer's father tried to get him treatment for his drinking but, as usual, Jeffrey Dahmer couldn't stick with this for very long. Aside from killing people, Dahmer could never seem to apply himself to anything.

(417) At the rate Dahmer's murders were escalating, it seems plausible to think that he would have murdered at least a dozen more people had he been left to his own devices for another year or two.

(418) Lionel Dahmer had what you might describe as slightly old-fashioned religious views on homosexuality. Nonetheless, he was calm and supportive when he found out that his son was gay.

(419) It is sometimes said that you don't get necrophile female serial killers like Dennis Nilsen or Jeffrey Dahmer but this isn't true at all. Female serial killers like Piroska Jancsó Ladányi, Guadalupe Martínez de Bejarano, and Jane Toppan were all sexually excited by dead bodies.

(420) Studies have shown that the average serial killer will kill four to five victims over an average period of six years.

(421) Dahmer apparently said that he fully expected to be killed by someone in prison. He was certainly right about that.

(422) Those who knew Dahmer say that he seemed to lack the

ability to laugh. The best he could do was smirk.

(423) In an interview in prison, Dahmer said his daily prison routine was breakfast, go back to bed, lunch, sleep again, dinner, and then watch television. He made prison sound quite nice!

(424) In 1992, Ambrosia closed and demolished their downtown Milwaukee chocolate factory and moved to a new more modern facility on the city's northwest side. The move was apparently long planned anyway but it was convenient timing because they obviously didn't want the chocolate factory where Dahmer had worked to become a ghoulish tourist attraction.

(425) There seem to be a large number of websites which have endless Jeffrey Dahmer jokes (mostly about cannibalism). You could probably say this is of questionable taste.

(426) Dahmer attended Hazel Harvey Elementary School in Barberton, OH.

(427) One of Dahmer's regular pranks at school was to trace the outline of a murder victim in chalk on the floor.

(428) Dahmer's original ambition in the army was to become a military policeman. He became a medic though instead.

(429) Dahmer picked up one of his victims at a gay pride parade.

(430) Serial killers often say that killing is very compulsive once they do it for the first time.

(431) Jeffrey Dahmer was 31 when he was arrested.

(432) Prior to Jeffrey Dahmer, Milwaukee was probably most famous for being where the sitcom Happy Days took place.

(433) Dahmer's lawyer and father thought he should have been sent to a psychiatric hospital rather than a prison.

(434) Dahmer, encouraged by his father, briefly had an interest in weightlifting and bodybuilding as a young man.

(435) In a prison interview, Jeffrey Dahmer denied the popular perception of him that he was shy. Dahmer didn't think he was especially shy at all.

(436) When he was at college, Jeffrey Dahmer frequently donated blood so he could get extra cash to buy booze.

(437) The police suspected that Dahmer had been eating some of his victims even before he told them. The reason for this is that they found literally no real food in his apartment at all when he was captured. All he had in the fridge was bags of human flesh. It wasn't unusual for Dahmer to have no food in the house though. He usually went out to fast food joints and diners for his meals. Dahmer's father said that when he visited his son there was usually nothing but milk and cans of soda in the fridge.

(438) The portable freezer in Dahmer's apartment contained 3480 g of human tissue when he was arrested.

(439) On August 5, 1991, a candlelight vigil was held in Milwaukee in memory of Dahmer's victims. This was a nice thing for the community to do.

(440) At the time of his capture, Dahmer had lost his job and was about to be kicked out of his apartment because he didn't have the rent. There is therefore a theory that Dahmer started eating human flesh to save money! This is not unheard of when it comes to serial killers. Joachim Kroll killed fourteen people in Germany between 1955 and 1976. When the police entered the apartment where Kroll lived there was a hand boiling in a pan of water and human flesh in the fridge. When he was asked to explain why he had eaten parts of his victims,

Kroll calmly replied that he had done this to reduce his supermarket shopping bills for food.

(441) In many ways, Dahmer moving into his own apartment was the worst thing that could have happened to him because he now had the freedom to invite people home and do with them as he pleased. His new independence also meant he had less contact with his family.

(442) The media even turned up at Dahmer's grandmother's house when his crimes came to light. The Dahmer family felt this was intrusive and over the top.

(443) Some people threw eggs at the house of Dahmer's elderly grandmother when he was arrested. This was completely ridiculous and cruel. Dahmer's grandmother obviously had nothing to do with his crimes.

(444) Dahmer's lawyer said that initially Jeffrey Dahmer didn't want any of his relatives to visit him in prison because he was ashamed of his crimes.

(445) When he was in prison, Dahmer got a lot of letters from people asking for his autograph. These people were obviously thinking of the monetary value a true crime artifact like this might fetch.

(446) Dahmer had a copy of the film Hellbound: Hellraiser II in his apartment when he was arrested.

(447) Dahmer was a fan of the band Def Leppard.

(448) It is sometimes reported that Jeffrey Dahmer was molested by a neighbour when he was about eight. Dahmer always denied that this story was true though.

(449) Kesha's 2010 song Cannibal was controversial because it mentioned Jeffrey Dahmer in the lyrics. The offending lines were - 'Your little heart goes pitter-patter, I want your liver on

a platter. Be too sweet and you'll be a goner, yeah, I'll pull a Jeffrey Dahmer. I eat boys up, breakfast and lunch, then when I'm thirsty, I drink their blood.
Carnivore, animal, I am a cannibal. I eat boys up, you better run.'

(450) A former residents of Oxford apartments where Dahmer lived said the whole building stank at the best of times so this probably mitigated some of the dreadful odours coming from Dahmer's apartment.

(451) The body of a murdered person was once found in one of the apartments in Dahmer's building while he lived there. Dahmer had nothing to do with this death.

(452) Jeffrey Dahmer has been referenced in more songs than any other serial killer. Around sixty or so. Not even Ted Bundy or Jack the Ripper can match this.

(453) A former neighbour of Dahmer said that he seemed to have a particular dislike for women.

(454) Dahmer believed in the occult and was certainly fascinated by it.

(455) Although there is no firm evidence that Dahmer ever killed very young children many true crime experts believe he was certainly capable of doing this.

(456) After the success of the Netflix drama Monster in 2022, there were appeals for people not to dress as Jeffrey Dahmer for Halloween. What would a Jeffrey Dahmer costume look like anyway? An orange boiler suit and a pair of aviator glasses?

(457) The sandwich shop that Dahmer worked in while he lived in Florida was also a pizza place. It could well be then that people in the area had a pizza delivered by Jeffrey Dahmer!

(458) Although their crimes were uncannily similar, Dahmer was nothing like Dennis Nilsen when it came to personality. Nilsen was abrasive, confident, and had a big ego. None of these qualities applied to Dahmer.

(459) There is no evidence that Dahmer was relieved to have been captured or wanted to be captured. The simple truth is that he simply became 'sloppy' in the end and this is how he was caught.

(460) Dahmer said it was difficult to get any sleep in prison because there was always someone screaming somewhere.

(461) You can, should you desire one, buy a Jeffrey Dahmer bookmark on Etsy.

(462) The journalist Nancy Glass interviewed Dahmer in prison a year before his death. Glass said the chilling thing about Dahmer is that he was so ordinary. She said he wouldn't have stood out in a crowd.

(463) Jeffrey Dahmer's trial was open to the public. That was doubtless why they had such stringent security measures.

(464) As you might well imagine, the polaroids Dahmer had taken of his victims were distressing and grim for the police to look at. One photograph had a victim in the bath with the chest and stomach sliced open.

(465) The police detectives who questioned Dahmer said he had an excellent memory. He could recall many intricate little details about his victims.

(466) Neighbours of Dahmer said that he usually smelled of booze when they encountered him in the hall.

(467) Lionel Dahmer said that when he picked his son up from college, Jeffrey Dahmer's bedroom shelf was full of empty beer and wine bottles.

(468) One of Dahmer's pranks at school was to 'photobomb' the National Honor Society group photo. They had to black Dahmer out of the photograph.

(469) Dahmer was a frequent patron of adult bookstores.

(470) At the time of his capture, Dahmer was killing victims at the rate of one a month.

(471) Billy Capshaw, the army medic who says Dahmer abused him in Germany, said he only dredged up the memories of this abuse through therapy and hypnosis.

(472) On average, Dahmer weighed about 180 pounds.

(473) When Dahmer was at Ohio State college he lived in Morril Tower - a hall of residence.

(474) Morril Tower is still there and students still live in Dahmer's old room.

(475) Dahmer's college room was a quad in that he had a bedroom but shared other facilities.

(476) Dahmer's roomates at college later said they had practically no memory of him at all. He rarely spoke to them and was either asleep or out on his own getting drunk.

(477) Dahmer's first victim Steven Hicks was on his way to a concert at Cleveland's Blossom Music Center at the time of his fateful meeting with Jeffrey Dahmer.

(478) Dahmer said that if he had found a submissive and obedient romantic partner who never left him he might not have killed. He basically wanted a loyal mindless sex slave who did whatever he wanted 24 hours a day. The type of person that Dahmer fantasised about though didn't actually exist in real life. Dahmer was dangerously delusional and the gulf between fantasy and reality became too much for him in the

end.

(479) It has been speculated that Dahmer might have murdered Steven Hicks because Hicks spurned his sexual advances. Dahmer denied this though and said he killed Hicks because he didn't want him to leave.

(480) Dahmer's army colleagues said he rarely spoke about his parents and even gave the impression that he didn't have a mother.

(481) Dahmer's mother Joyce was irritated by Lionel Dahmer's memoir because it was rather critical of her.

(482) Dahmer didn't have much contact at all with his mother in the 1980s.

(483) Dahmer seemed to have a peculiar sexual fetish for skulls.

(484) The Ambassador Hotel, where Dahmer killed Steven Tuomi, was a very cheap hotel when Dahmer stayed there. It has undergone a lot of renovations and is felt to be much nicer now.

(485) Özgür Dengiz was known as the Turkish Jeffrey Dahmer. Özgür Dengiz killed two people and attempted to kill another. His crimes took place from 1997 to 2007. When he was captured, Dengiz was found to have human flesh in his fridge. Dengiz said he liked human flesh so much he would even eat it raw.

(486) Jeffrey Dahmer trained as an army medical specialist at Fort Sam Houston in San Antonio, Texas. The ironic thing about Dahmer is that he was trained to saved lives but was more interested in taking them.

(487) The German police retrospectively investigated Dahmer for the murder of a ten year-old boy which occurred while he

was in Germany. The police in Germany found though that there was no connection between Dahmer and this tragic unsolved murder.

(488) Dahmer was a fan of the band Iron Maiden.

(489) Billy Capshaw, the army medic who says Dahmer abused him in Germany, said that Dahmer was always drinking vodka & orange.

(490) The Campus Circle Project purchased the 49-unit building Dahmer's apartment resided in for $325,000. They helped to rehouse the residents before it was demolished.

(491) The true crime figure most famously associated with necrophilia is Ed Gein. In 1957, Plainfield hardware store owner Bernice Worden vanished. The police deduced from cash register receipts that Ed Gein had been one of the last visitors to the store so they went to his farm. At the farm they found the body of Worden decapitated and hung up like a deer. It turned out too that Ed Gein had been digging up bodies from the local cemetery and making masks, furniture, and skin suits from them. At Gein's farm, the police also found the head of a woman named Mary Hogan who had been missing for three years. Gein used female genitalia in some of the bric-a-brac around his home. He'd also fashioned some skulls into serving bowls. Gein was one of the first killers to gain national attention in America. His crimes were so bizarre that a morbid public and media fascination with the case was probably unavoidable.

(492) Oxford Apartments, where Dahmer lived, had a cream exterior.

(493) Dahmer killed Steven Tuomi in room 507 of the Ambassador Hotel. You can stay in this room today if you book it.

(494) Dahmer said he killed Ernest Miller with a knife because the victim was not only strong but regaining consciousness as

the effects of the drugged drink wore off.

(495) One of Dahmer's friends at high school said that when it came to light that he was a serial killer cannibal, all the things Dahmer had done at school to amuse them no longer seemed funny anymore and now simply came across as sinister in retrospect.

(496) It is believed that many serial killers like to strangle their victims because they want the murder to feel intimate.

(497) Dahmer said that he took several men back to his grandmother's house without killing them. Dahmer said he only killed the 'special' ones.

(498) Katy Perry was criticised for a lyric in her 2013 track Dark Horse referencing Dahmer. The lyric (by a guest rapper) was as follows - "She eats your heart out like Jeffrey Dahmer (whoa!)."

(499) Dahmer put on weight when he was arrested and sent to prison. Poverty had malnourished him on the outside but in prison he got three meals a day.

(500) At the start of the trial, Dahmer's lawyer reminded the jury that this case was not about homosexuality or race. It was essentially about whether or not Dahmer was sane or insane.

(501) Hollywood often depicts serial killers as elusive criminal masterminds who are always two steps ahead of the police. The reality is very different. Most serial killers are not exactly impossible to catch.

(502) Dahmer only spent one semester in college.

(503) Someone who vaguely knew Dahmer at college later said that she once saw him passed out in the street drunk near the campus.

(504) Dahmer said he once went home with a man after a boozy night at the 219 Club and woke up to find himself 'hogtied'. Dahmer said he asked to be let down and untied and then left. Dahmer said he later discovered a large section of a candle had been stuck up his bottom during this encounter (of which he had little memory).

(505) There is an urban myth that the film director John Waters purchased Dahmer's fridge. John Waters was more credibly alleged though to have owned a John Wayne Gacy painting.

(506) There is usually a 'cooling off' period after a serial killer murders for the first time. This certainly applied to Dahmer.

(507) When the trial began, Dahmer's lawyer warned the jury that they were "Going to hear about things you probably didn't know existed in the real world."

(508) Tracy Edwards became something of a celebrity for a time after he escaped from Dahmer. He even appeared on The Phil Donahue show.

(509) It was obviously a lot easier for Dahmer to dispose of victims when he lived with his father and then his grandmother. He had easy quick access to woodland and relative privacy. When he moved to an apartment and started killing people it obviously became a lot more complicated to dispose of remains - hence the nightmarish situation he ended up in.

(510) The death metal band Macabre wrote an album titled 'Dahmer'.

(511) Prison cigarette restrictions were lifted for Jeffrey Dahmer during his interviews with detectives because the authorities believed he'd be more willing and able to talk at length if he was allowed to smoke.

(512) In his confession, Jeffrey Dahmer said that when he cut up his victims and place the victim in a tub. It became a very precise sort of ritual.

(513) Reginald Oates is an American killer who killed four young boys within the span of two days in April 1968, in Baltimore, Maryland. Oates had sex with the bodies of the victims after their death. When he was captured he had body parts (including genitals) from the murdered victims in a bag. Oates was deemed too insane to stand trial and sent to the Clifton T. Perkins State Hospital in Jessup. Some would contend that Dahmer should have ended up in a similar place.

(514) We tend to think that necrophile serial killers only get a few days of sexual gratification out of the bodies because of decomposition. This wasn't really the case with Dahmer though because he continued to get sexual gratification out of the bones, heads, and even the photographs.

(515) Dahmer said that his personal hygiene, thanks to his frazzled mental state, began to slip circa 1986, and he found it a struggle to do normal things like shave and wash his clothes.

(516) Wendy Patrickus, who was one of Dahmer's lawyers, had to visit his apartment when it was still an active crime scene. She said she vomited afterwards.

(517) Some of the polaroids of Dahmer's dead victims found in his flat included Dahmer's leg or foot in the photo from where he was standing over them.

(518) The police detectives who interviewed Dahmer after his capture said that it took him a long time to relax in their presence. They basically had to be polite and patient with him and build up his trust.

(519) Dahmer always watched Gilligan`s Island when he was a kid.

(520) Dr Park Dietz, a prosecution witness at the trial, said that Dahmer wanted to 'freeze dry' his victims but couldn't work out how to do this.

(521) Dahmer told the police that he got no enjoyment from the act of killing his victims. It is debatable if this is true. Dahmer sometimes contradicted himself in interviews. This is why some question whether or not he was a truly reliable narrator.

(522) Dr Park Dietz, a prosecution witness at the trial, said that Dahmer's sexuality was just a coincidence. What he presumably meant by this is that if Dahmer had been straight he'd STILL be a killer but murdering women instead of men.

(523) Dahmer wanted to have blue strobe lights at the creepy altar of skulls he planned to build.

(524) In the Netflix show Monster, Glenda Cleveland is depicted as living next door to Dahmer but in reality she didn't even live in the same building.

(525) According to the press, Dahmer was suspended from his position as a prison janitor in 1993 for impersonating a member of staff on the telephone. Dahmer was still a prankster - even now.

(526) Those who interviewed Dahmer in custody say he said that he'd always had a strange (and ultimately mistaken) belief that he would never be caught.

(527) Though Dahmer expressed some remorse for his crimes, a number of experts doubt that serial killers are truly capable of this emotion.

(528) Bridget Geiger said that Jeffrey Dahmer apologised to her for disappearing at the prom.

(529) Dahmer's complete police confession was 160 pages

long.

(530) Dahmer said in an interview that he could never manage to get 'gruesome and horrible' thoughts out of his head.

(531) West Allis, Wisconsin, where Dahmer lived with his grandmother, was the birthplace of the famous entertainer Liberace.

(532) Dahmer said that his knowledge of human anatomy came from reading and also his medic training in the army.

(533) Dahmer told the police that he sometimes ate the thigh 'meat' of his victims.

(534) People in Dahmer's apartment building apparently found him pleasant enough on the rare occasion that they spoke to him.

(535) Dahmer said there was a gap between his first and second murder because he had been spooked and scared by the incident where the cops pulled him over when he still had victim parts in the car.

(536) Dahmer had some griffin figurines in his apartment when he was arrested. In medieval heraldry, the griffin became a Christian symbol of divine power and a guardian of the divine.

(537) Dahmer said that when the griffin figurines were knocked off his table the night Tracy Edwards escaped he knew that he was doomed. It was a bad omen.

(538) Dahmer apparently owned some bicycles.

(539) Dahmer slipped out of college for the last time without saying goodbye to a single person.

(540) It appears that most of Dahmer's relatives suspected he

was gay even they knew for sure. The fact that he never had girlfriends and only brought men home was obviously a bit of a giveaway.

(541) Statistics indicate that insanity pleas in serial killer cases are generally unsuccessful. It is very difficult to prove that someone was so mentally impaired they didn't know what they were doing when they killed people.

(542) After Dahmer was captured, the police in California investigated whether he was connected to the discovery of a foot and body parts in Fresno. It turned out he wasn't.

(543) Dahmer looks uncannily like the boxing trainer Teddy Atlas in some of his old photographs!

(544) Bridget Geiger said that the teenage Dahmer was very 'nerdy' and a complete outcast at school.

(545) Lionel Dahmer appeared on The Oprah Winfrey Show in 1994. He said that since Jeffrey Dahmer's arrest he had got closer to his son. He said he would never abandon 'Jeff' and always visit him in prison.

(546) Dahmer said that going out on the 'hunt' for victims was a big part of the 'thrill' of being a serial killer.

(547) Dahmer was said by fellow students to have got no mail while he was at college.

(548) A nurse who had to give Dahmer medical training when he was an army recruit later said it was darkly ironic that a man with no empathy whatsoever was assigned to become an army medic.

(549) Morril Tower, where Dahmer briefly lived as a student, is a 23 floor building.

(550) Some of the disturbing polaroids Dahmer took of his

victims made their way to TikTok recently - which created some controversy as users were doing 'reaction videos' to them.

(551) Some scenes for the film My Friend Dahmer were shot at Dahmer's real childhood home.

(552) In 2022, the NY Post reported that Dahmer's childhood home was now valued at $372,000.

(553) After he released his book A Father's story, Lionel Dahmer was sued by some of relatives of the victims for invasion of privacy.

(554) At the trial, the uncle of victim Ernest Miller said that Jeffrey Dahmer was the 'perfect candidate' for the death penalty.

(555) Bridget Geiger said that the teenage Dahmer was 'scared to death' of girls and wanted nothing to do with them.

(556) A former neighbour who knew Dahmer when he was a boy said he always seemed to be a lonely child with no friends.

(557) Dahmer said that the first kill of any serial killer is the one that is most vividly ingrained in the memory.

(558) One of Dahmer's neighbours was once briefly in his apartment and inquired about the big blue barrel which mysteriously sat in the corner. Dahmer quickly changed the subject.

(559) Dahmer said of his knowledge of pills used to sedate people came from his army medic training.

(560) Dahmer killed for the first time only a few weeks after graduating from high school.

(561) There is an 'underground' comic book called Jeffrey

Dahmer vs. Jesus Christ. You haven't missed much if you've never read this book.

(562) Dahmer had a mustache in his younger years.

(563) Dahmer had a lava lamp in his apartment.

(564) Tracy Edwards, who escaped from Dahmer and sealed his fate, told the media that he knew a bit of karate and thinks this helped him to get away from Dahmer.

(565) Sari Dahmer said they'd had a few weird incidents involving 'Jeff' at his grandmother's house which made them wonder what he was up to. There were bad odours and strange melted substances in the basement.

(566) The process of identifying Dahmer's victims was a long and complex operation. It was also a grim and upsetting task for all involved.

(567) The people most safe from Jeffrey Dahmer were women. Dahmer told the police he'd never had any interest at all in killing women.

(568) Bridget Geiger said that, a few months after their prom date, Dahmer told her he was gay. It was rare for him to reveal this to anyone but he clearly trusted and liked Bridget.

(569) People who knew Dahmer at the chocolate factory told the media that he was always quite affable - if quiet. They certainly hadn't detected anything dark or dangerous about him.

(570) Dahmer's former school principal said that Jeffrey Dahmer was always something of a puzzling mystery. As evidence of this he cited the fact that Dahmer got his highest and lowest grades in the SAME subject!

(571) The police had to search the land around Oxford

Apartments in case Dahmer had hidden any human remains there.

(572) A former neighbour of Dahmer said he always looked a bit dirty and in need of a shower.

(573) The manager of Dahmer's apartment building described Jeffrey Dahmer as a loner but not someone who caused any problems. He said Dahmer always paid his rent on time.

(574) Residents of Oxford Apartments said that Dahmer stood out like a sore thumb because he was practically the only white person who lived there.

(575) A person in Milwaukee created controversy after Dahmer's capture by having a Halloween display fashioned after the Jeffrey Dahmer crime scene.

(576) Jeffrey Dahmer's social security number was 249-60-3333.

(577) Dahmer repeatedly told the police that if he had really killed Adam Walsh he would have confessed.

(578) Dahmer, unlike Ted Bundy, did not try and blame pornography for the way his life had turned out.

(579) Musician Chris Butler bought Dahmer's childhood home in 2005. He said to a newspaper - "The house has a great vibe, I mean, after all, the house didn't kill anybody, and I don't believe in ghosts, and there's absolutely no reason to think there's anything untoward here."

(580) When he was in prison, Dahmer told the authorities that he had been sent letters from other killers who had yet to be captured.

(581) Dahmer told the police that he always had a recurring nightmare about a tornado chasing him.

(582) Dahmer said that viewing photographs of his victims and keeping their skulls was a way to try and stave off his urge to kill someone new.

(583) One of Dahmer's tax return forms can sell for $500 on true crime collectibles sites.

(584) When he was in prison, Dahmer said - 'This is the grand finale of a life poorly spent and the end result is just overwhelmingly depressing. A sick pathetic, miserable life story, that's all it is.'

(585) Around the time that Dahmer's trial began there was a newspaper article which claimed Dahmer had eaten his cellmate in prison. This story was obviously not true at all. Jeffrey Dahmer found this article funny when it was shown to him.

(586) In a prison interview, Dahmer said his sexuality had caused him a lot of problems. He said he didn't like being gay but there was nothing he could do to change that.

(587) Jeffrey Dahmer features in the 2011 horror sequel Gingerdead Man 3: Saturday Night Cleaver.

(588) Wendy Patrickus, who was one of Dahmer's lawyers, said she got death threats for representing him.

(589) A prison system spokesman said Dahmer usually sat up until 4am watching television.

(590) Forensic psychiatrist Carl Wahlstrom, who interviewed Dahmer four times, said that Dahmer believed his 'temple of skulls' would allow him to tap into positive energy and give him success in the real estate market.

(591) Dahmer loved playing with Lego as a kid.

(592) The Chicago Tribune reported in 1991 that Dahmer

surprised everyone in court because he seemed so polite and normal. He didn't look like a cannibal serial killer.

(593) When he was captured, Dahmer told the police he was very surprised that the residents in his building hadn't deduced anything because his apartment was really starting to stink.

(594) Tracy Edwards said that Dahmer began doing some weird ritual chant before he managed to escape.

(595) One factor in why Dahmer wasn't declared insane by the authorities is that his murders, for the most part, did not seem to be impulsive. There was a patent degree of calculation and preparation on Dahmer's part when he killed someone.

(596) A library card was found in Dahmer's apartment. He hadn't used it much though.

(597) Dahmer said he was guilty about the murders he committed. It's probably fair to say few believed him on this.

(598) Among the famous people who, like Jeffrey Dahmer, went to Ohio State University, are Jesse Owens, Harlan Ellison, Patricia Heaton, Richard Lewis, J. K. Simmons, and the golfer Jack Nicklaus.

(599) Billy Capshaw, the army medic who says Dahmer abused him in Germany, said Dahmer would lock him in their room as part of his dominating conduct.

(600) The prison authorities said that, contrary to what he might have claimed, Christopher Scarver had little to no contact with Dahmer before he murdered him.

(601) Dahmer had some Miller Light beer in his kitchen when he was arrested.

(602) Dahmer said that after he killed one of his victims he bit

the neck as a sort of vampiric experiment. It wasn't something he made a habit of though.

(603) There were 16 gallons of hydrochloric acid in Dahmer's apartment when he was arrested.

(604) Jeffrey Dahmer was apparently a frequent visitor to his local McDonalds. He didn't really cook much at home.

(605) Dahmer knew what he was doing was wrong but his only concern was to 'own' a person who could never leave him. In his disturbed mind the means justified the end.

(606) FBI Serial Crime Unit chief John Douglas once estimated there were around 25 to 50 active serial killers in the United States. This felt to many to be a rather conservative estimate.

(607) Dahmer said that when he lived with his grandmother he would cut up his victims while she was at church.

(608) After he was arrested the police asked Dahmer if he was relieved to have been caught. Dahmer said he wasn't relieved at all as he'd enjoyed his serial killer activities.

(609) Dahmer scuffled a little bit with the police officers who arrested him but he didn't put up a huge amount of resistance in the end.

(610) FBI Investigator Robert Ressler is often credited with coining the term serial killer. The term only really entered the general lexicon in the 1980s. The FBI generally states that one must kill three people to qualify as a serial killer. There must also be a gap between each killing. A bomber, for example, is a mass murderer or terrorist as opposed to a serial killer.

(611) Dahmer's college roommates suspected him of stealing from them. Dahmer apparently took stolen items to the pawnshop to fund his drinking.

(612) When he worked at the chocolate factory Dahmer would usually get home at eight in the morning. He would get a few hours sleep and then go out and have some lunch in the town. Dahmer liked simple fast food like burgers and fried chicken.

(613) Dahmer's tactics with victims was to avoid confrontation or a struggle. He sedated them so they could be killed when they were vulnerable and unable to offer resistance.

(614) Neighbours of Dahmer say they could often hear drilling coming from his apartment. They just presumed he was putting up some shelves or something.

(615) One of the disturbing polaroids found in Dahmer's apartment was of a human head in his sink with two severed hands next to it.

(616) Ted Bundy said that serial murder was really about possession and dominance rather than violence or lust.

(617) Serial killers tend to broadly fall into two categories - organised and disorganised. Organised serial killers are the ones who maintain a job and might even have an unsuspecting wife and children. Disorganised serial killers on the other hand are completely detached from society. One might argue that Dahmer fell somewhat in the middle of these categories in that he (mostly) held down a job but was alienated from society in his private life.

(618) Dahmer didn't create too much trouble in prison. He kept his head down and did his time.

(619) There is sometimes a mistaken tendency to think that a disproportionate percentage of serial killers are gay. This is probably a consequence of famous gay serial killers like Dennis Nilsen, Jeffrey Dahmer, and John Wayne Gacy. Studies show though that the overwhelming majority of serial killers are heterosexual. This tends to make the most notorious gay serial killers more famous. They aren't quite as common.

(620) Unlike other members of the family, Lionel Dahmer did not change his name when his son's crimes came to light. Lionel Dahmer said that he'd done nothing wrong himself so saw no reason to change his name in shame.

(621) In 2018, it was estimated that the United States had produced 2743 serial killers in its history.

(622) Dahmer had previously sexually assaulted the brother of his murder victim Konerak Sinthasomphone. This was just a strange coincidence. Dahmer didn't know these victims were related.

(623) The preserved skull and genitals of Dahmer's fifth victim Anthony Lee Sears were found in a filing cabinet following Dahmer's arrest in 1991.

(624) The 1970s saw a serial killer 'explosion' in America. Theories on this include mind-altering drugs and the trauma of Vietnam (neither of which applied to Dahmer). It could be though that there was simply more media reporting of such crimes.

(625) The most common unskilled serial killer occupation according to studies is general labourer. Dahmer fell into this category.

(626) One of Dahmer's childhood friends said that Jeffrey Dahmer used to like to visit graveyards at night.

(627) When he was in prison in 1989, another inmate claimed that Dahmer said he hated black people and wanted to kill them all.

(628) Dahmer was an unusual sort of serial killer in that the actual murder was the least important part to him. It was what came AFTER the murder that interested him.

(629) The strange thing about serial killers is that a number of

them have a superficial charm. They can often blend into society and seem ordinary.

(630) Lionel Dahmer said that when he first heard about what his son had done his first thought was that his son must have had some dominating accomplice who made him do these awful things.

(631) Dahmer took part in a séance when he was in high school.

(632) Jeffrey Dahmer was fond of fishing when he was younger.

(633) A book that Dahmer read a lot as a child was Alfred Hitchcock Presents Ghost Stories for Young People.

(634) Dahmer's father found out about the stolen mannequin and asked his son why he had stolen it. Jeffrey Dahmer said that he just did it for a prank. That was obviously not the real truth.

(635) The profile of Dahmer's victims was unusual because serial killers typically murder the opposite sex within their own ethnic group.

(636) Jeffrey Dahmer was diagnosed with borderline personality disorder, schizotypal personality disorder, and a psychotic disorder.

(637) Dahmer's father Lionel said that when he first went back to work after his son's crimes were uncovered, work colleagues didn't really know what to say to him or how to react.

(638) There was no real food in Dahmer's apartment when he was arrested but he did have some Doritos and Ruffles potato chips in the kitchen.

(639) When he was prison, people sent Dahmer all sorts of

stuff. He was sent cans of food, stuffed animal toys, vitamin pills, and religious books. He wasn't allowed to keep much of it though.

(640) Dahmer victim Tony Hughes was deaf.

(641) In the Netflix drama Monster, Christopher Scarver is shown researching Jeffery Dahmer in the library to find out what he did. This is pure fiction. Scarver would have been well aware who Dahmer was without having to do research. Dahmer was all over the television news and papers.

(642) Billy Capshaw, the army medic who says Dahmer abused him in Germany, says he is pretty sure Dahmer drugged him more than once. Capshaw said he woke up one day and found himself tied to a bed.

(643) A report once found that 42% of necrophiles had murdered someone to obtain a body with which to act out their desires.

(644) Lionel Dahmer believes that the many pills and prescriptions that his former wife was on when she was pregnant might have been a factor in why his son turned out the way he did.

(645) Jeffrey Dahmer had some similarities with another 80s serial killer called Bob Berdella. Berdella restrained, tortured, and killed at least six men from 1984 to 1987 in Kansas City, Missouri. He was known as The Kansas City Butcher. Berdella deduced he was gay from a very young age but he struggled to come to terms with his sexuality and didn't admit to it for a long time. As a teenager he even had a few girlfriends in an attempt to disguise his real self. His father died when he was a relatively young man and this is said to have made him even more aloof and withdrawn. Berdella didn't like the fact that his mother then remarried. Berdella's hobbies were collecting stamps, strange art, and antiques.

In the early eighties he used his collection to start a business. Berdella ran a booth at a market called Bob's Bizarre Bizarre which sold oddities and antiques. It is sometimes suggested that he might sold some of the skulls of his victims at this booth. Berdella studied art at college but dropped out in the end. During this period he was busted on drugs charges a few times. One of the drugs he used was the mind altering LSD. Despite this, Berdella seemed - on the outside - to be doing quite well. He was popular in the community in which he lived and, in addition to the business he started, got work as a chef. Berdella seemed to befriend a lot of runaways and male prostitutes. He claimed to be a sort of mentor to them and said he was helping them with drug addictions. The police later deduced that Berdella wasn't quite so generous as he claimed in his relationships with these young men. They believe he was exploiting them for sex.

By now, Berdella was pretty open about his sexuality and most people he knew were aware that he was gay. Berdella murdered for the first time in 1984. His victims were all young men that he had gained the trust of and then isolated. The murders were very sadistic - even for a serial killer. Berdella would drug and restrain the victims and then basically torture them for as long as they could survive. The victims were raped, cut, given electric shocks, and he would even inject them with cleaning fluids in the neck so they couldn't scream. Berdella would often the break the bones of the victims' hands with an iron bar so that they couldn't put up a struggle. Berdella claimed to have been influenced by the 1965 film The Collector (which adapted a novel by John Fowles) - where an alienated young man is obsessed by a female student and makes her a captive in his cellar. He wanted his victims to become compliant and trust him. However, most of them died from torture long before they got anywhere near this stage. Berdella's disturbing activities came to an end in 1988 when a male prostitute named Christopher Bryson, after days of torture, managed to ecape from Berdella's home and run across the street (in a dog collar). He found some police and told them what had happened. The badly injured Bryson was taken to hospital and the police evenually obtained permision to search Berdella's home. They found that he had an elaborate torture room but the worst was yet to come. They also found human skulls and a human head. There was a chainsaw covered in human blood and various body parts. The police also found photographs Berdella had taken of his victims in various stages of torture. Berdella had also written detailed diaries of his torture methods.

Berdella was sentenced to life imprisonment without the possibility of parole. He had to do a plea bargain to avoid the death penalty. This involved a full confession in order to help identify all of his victims. Berdella was the worst sort of serial killer in that he was more interested in torture than death. He would keep his victims alive as long as he could before he killed them or they died. Berdella never seemed to express much remorse for his terrible crimes. When he was in prison he complained that the authorities withheld his medication for high blood pressure. He died of a heart attack in 1992 at the age of 43. It's safe to say that no one had much sympathy when they heard he had died. Berdella's disposal of his victims was similar to Dahmer in that he dismembered them and put body parts in the trash. Berdella also had a head in his freezer and liked to take photographs of his victims. These killers shared the same sexuality and many traits but the key difference was that Berdella was into torture and Dahmer into necrophilia. They both clearly though, through different approaches, liked to exert complete control over victims.

(646) It has been alleged that Dahmer had some indecent exposure incidents with local children when he was in Germany but the army covered this up.

(647) Students at Ohio State have claimed that Jeffrey Dahmer's ghost haunts his old halls of residence Morrill Tower.

(648) Believe it or not, in the United States and most European countries there are no laws against the consumption

of human flesh. However, you can obviously be prosecuted for murder, desecration, and necrophilia so being a cannibal WILL land you in prison.

(649) Another notorious cannibal killer was Nikolai Espolovich Dzhumagaliev. Nikolai Espolovich Dzhumagaliev was a Soviet serial killer who was convicted of seven murders commited from 1979 to 1980. He is known as Kolya the Maneater because he ate the flesh of some of his victims. Of his first murder, Dzhumagaliev told the police -

"I cut the corpse's breast into strips, removed the ovaries, and separated the pelvis and hips; I then put these pieces into a backpack and carried them home. I melted the fat to fry with, and some parts I pickled. Once, I put the parts through a meat grinder and made dumplings. I saved the meat for myself; I never served it to anyone else. Twice, I grilled parts—the heart and the kidneys. Grilled meat, too. But it was tough, and I had to cook it for a long time in its own fat. The meat of this woman took me a month to eat. The first time I ate human flesh, I had to force myself, but then I got used to it."

(650) When he was at school and college, Dahmer's method for concealing alcohol in class was to slip some in an empty soda can.

(651) Cannibals go way back in true crime. Alferd Packer was known as The Colorado Cannibal. He was a prospector and murderer who ate human flesh to survive in the wilderness in 1874. He was later captured and imprisoned. Even further back in 1830, a criminal named Edward Broughton was transported from England to Tasmania (then known as Van Diemen's Land) in Australia to work in a penal colony. Broughton ended up on a work party of five convicts. There was only one police constable in charge of the party and the prisoners attacked him and escaped. The men had an axe (which they had stolen from their work party) and trekked through the wilderness in search of food. They were eventually exhausted and starving. Broughton decided they would simply

have to eat one of the convicts. As a consequence, Richard Hutchinson (who was convicted for horse theft) was murdered by Broughton with the axe and his body was roasted over a fire.

Broughton made a pact with a teenage convict in the party named Patrick Fagan. They both watched over one another while the other was asleep. Broughton kept a firm grip on the precious axe. The axe gave him power over the group. William Coventry, the oldest of the convicts, was chosen to be the next victim when they ran out of food again. He was killed with the axe and his flesh roasted over another fire. The men ate as much as they could and then stuffed the remaining human flesh in their pockets for later. The convicts continued their trek and thoughts turned to who would be next to eat. Broughton was asked to kill Fagan but he refused to allow the death his friend. The matter was taken out of his own hands though when one of the remaining convicts named Matthew Macavoy murdered Fagan with the axe when Broughton was asleep. Broughton and Macavoy cooked the body and had a large meal. Broughton and Macavoy gave themselves up a few days later when they reached an outpost. In 1832 they were hung for murder and cannibalism. Broughton made a full confession.

(652) Tracy Edwards said that Dahmer swung a knife at him as he fled from the apartment.

(653) It has been speculated that Dahmer was able to hide his sexuality so well because he wasn't a 'camp' or effeminate person at all.

(654) Rolf Mueller was the police officer who first discovered that Dahmer had body parts, bones, flesh, and heads all over his apartment. "You think you've seen it all out here, and then something like this happens," Mueller later told a newspaper.

(655) Judith Becker, a University of Arizona clinical psychologist who spent two days interviewing Dahmer,

testified that Dahmer told her he preferred comatose sex partners to dead ones.

(656) Many felt that the Dennis Nilsen trial indicated that definitions of sanity and diminished responsibility needed to be looked at again. While it was true that Nilsen was aware of what he had done and seemed 'normal' in person it would be ludicrous all the same to call him sane given his crimes. You could say the same thing about Jeffrey Dahmer. Dahmer was declared sane by the authorities - despite killing people, keeping their heads in the fridge, and eating human flesh.

(657) Dahmer's mother Joyce turned down a $10,000 offer from a tabloid to do a short interview about her son. She thought it would be wrong to use the tragedy to make money.

(658) Jeffrey Dahmer would sometimes try to persuade himself that he hadn't hurt his victims because they were dead or unconscious when he did all the bad stuff. This is what you might call a cognitive distortion.

(659) Dahmer featured on the episode of South Park titled Hell on Earth 2006.

(660) The surname Dahmer is German in terms of origin and ancestry.

(661) Our morbid obsession with cannibalism in true crime stems from the fact that eating human flesh is seen as the ultimate taboo.

(662) When he was asked about the race of his victims, Dahmer said he did not go out seeking black men but simply zeroed in on the best looking men he could realistically get to come home with him. In most cases these men obviously turned out to be black.

(663) Letters sent to Dahmer in prison can sell for $100 on true crime collectibles sites.

(664) A period authentic chocolate wrapper from the factory where Dahmer worked can sell for $140 online.

(665) Dahmer told the police that he had to put up with his bosses telling him what to do at work but he would not put up with anyone telling him what to do in his private life. He had to have complete control over that.

(666) Dahmer said that before prison he had never thought about suicide.

(667) Another notorious cannibal killer was Peter Bryan. Bryan was a killer who murdered three people in England from 1993 to 2004. When he was captured by the police in 2004, Bryan was cooking parts of a victim's brain in a frying pan. "I ate his brains with butter," Bryan told the police. "It was really nice." Bryan was completely insane. He was sent to Broadmoor Hospital - where he later killed another inmate because he said he wanted to eat more human flesh.

(668) There have been some great serial killer films but you do have to sift through a lot of dreck to get to them. The general rule is to avoid the straight to DVD horror cheapies as they tend to be awful. The television films and television dramas based on serial killers are usually vastly superior and many of these are well worth watching.

(669) One other factor why there are less serial killers today is there are more social interventions. This might have saved some serial killers of the past by taking them out of society and treating them before they became killers. We like to think that mental health and social care is something that has come on leaps and bounds in recent years. Maybe, just maybe, someone like a Jeffrey Dahmer, if he was a teenager today, might have been diagnosed and looked after before he began to spiral out of control.

(670) One contributing factor as to why Dahmer was discharged from the army, besides his drinking problem, is

that he had a bad shoulder which hampered his ability to perform his duties.

(671) Dahmer was said to be irritated that the press sometimes reported his murders as racially motivated hate crimes.

(672) Dahmer told the police that even if he had been offered professional help for his personal demons in the past he would not have taken up this offer.

(673) Dahmer told the police that killing someone and abusing the body only satisfied him for a few months at best. Once that time had elapsed he had an uncontrollable urge to kill again.

(674) Dahmer said he kept the body of Tony Hughes in his bed for three days.

(675) A photo of Dahmer's police mug shot can sell for about $50 online.

(676) You can buy an 18" Demented Dollz Dahmer Plush Doll online. The doll is holding a spatula and fork.

(677) The police found a gay porn film on the floor of Dahmer's bedroom. The film was called Be My Baby. In those days films were VHS tapes.

(678) A copy of the graphic novel My Friend Dahmer signed by the author can sell for over $100 online.

(679) When Dahmer was killed in prison, a newspaper had the headline 'The Silence of the Damned'.

(680) A photograph of Dahmer as a baby can sell for $600 on true crime collectibles sites.

(681) Dahmer was put on prozac in prison.

(682) One of the reasons why Dahmer got fired from the

chocolate factory is that his attendance became inconsistent because he had to spend more and more time at home disposing of his victims.

(683) Dahmer was said to feel bad about the fact that he'd made Milwaukee famous for all the wrong reasons.

(684) Dahmer said he made an effort to stop killing after his second murder but, alas, he wasn't able to do this.

(685) A court clerk at the Dahmer trial later sued the city of Milwaukee for $65,000 in 1997 for the psychological trauma she'd endured working that case.

(686) Dahmer's stepmother said he was a gentle person when sober but became scary when he was drunk.

(687) American killers seem to have the freedom (whether one agrees with this practice or not) to conduct prison interviews much more than their British counterparts. You can find prison interviews with everyone from Ted Bundy to Jeffrey Dahmer if you look. However, you'll never find a prison interview with Peter Sutcliffe or Ian Huntley. As for Dennis Nilsen, he only got a few minutes on television. American serial killers are interviewed much more than British ones. They are allowed to become dark celebrities. This was clearly a source of irritation to Dennis Nilsen. His ego would have loved the chance to appear on television all the time.

(688) There was only one solitary black person on the jury at Dahmer's trial.

(689) Dahmer said he felt a sense of relief when his victims were dead because it meant he didn't have to worry about their needs or concerns anymore.

(690) There was a leak of some of Dahmer's victim polaroids on Reddit. They were certainly not for the faint of heart.

(691) Dahmer told the police that by retaining the skulls he felt the death of his victim was not a 'total loss'. What he meant by this is that he had managed to retain a part of them which he could keep.

(692) Jeffrey is a name deriving from German and English origin. The name translates to "pledge of peace" or "God's peace".

(693) The Jeffrey Dahmer 'action figure' made by Spectre Studios can sell for $300 these days.

(694) Dahmer featured on the Devil's Night and Be Our Guest episodes of American Horror Story.

(695) When he was in prison, Dahmer told his mother that he still had an urge to kill and was therefore glad he was locked up.

(696) Dennis Nilsen (who was plainly wrong about this) didn't actually believe that Jeffrey Dahmer was really a cannibal. "He is talking subconsciously. It's a kind of wishful thinking," said Nilsen. "What he really wants is spiritual ingestion, to take the essence of the person into himself and thereby feel bigger. It's almost a paternal thing, in an odd way."

(697) Captured serial killers often like to hold onto some secrets and be cryptic about what they know because this is their only way to retain some sense of power. This didn't seem to apply to Jeffrey Dahmer.

(698) Army colleagues said that Dahmer was a fan of the screen comedian W.C Fields.

(699) Killers as crazy as Dahmer are by no means uncommon around the world. Zhang Yongming was a Chinese serial killer responsible for at least eleven murders from 2008 to 2012. He sold the flesh of his victims at a local market and pretended it was ostrich meat. When he was arrested, the police found that

Yongming had preserved human eyeballs in jars. The flesh of his victims was hanging up to dry.

(700) There is an urban myth at Ohio State State University that Dahmer used Mirror Lake to dispose of victims. Mirror Lake is a picturesque pond on the campus.

(701) Dahmer never officially declared a major when he was briefly at college.

(702) Believe it or not, Dahmer is not the only serial killer to have attended Ohio State Univirsity. Michael Swango also went there. Swango (born 1954) is a former physician estimated to have been involved in as many as sixty deadly poisonings of patients and colleagues. He was sentenced in 2000 to three consecutive life terms.

(703) Dahmer's apartment was only a few blocks from the Ambassador Hotel - where he killed Steven Tuomi.

(704) Dahmer told the police that the copious sleeping pills he used to drug his victims were obtained from a Dr Hong. To be fair to the doctor in question, he obviously had no idea what these prescribed pills were ACTUALLY being used for!

(705) The word "cannibalism" comes from the name that the Spanish gave to the Caribs (Caníbales). The ironic thing is that the Caribs were not even cannibals.

(706) Dorángel Vargas was another true crime cannibal. Dorángel Vargas was known as The Hannibal Lecter of the Andes. He killed at least fourteen people in the mid 1990s in Venezuela. Vargas was homeless and preyed on victims in a local park. He confessed to eating eleven of his victims. Vargas said he did not eat women or children because they were too pure. He also declined to eat overweight people because he said fatty flesh was less healthy.

(707) Dahmer was discharged from the army in 1981 under

Chapter 9 of Army Regulation 635–200. This regulation pertained to substance (specifically alcohol in this case) abuse.

(708) Billy Capshaw, the army medic who says Dahmer abused him in Germany, claims that Dahmer would sometimes return to the barracks late at night covered in blood. Capshaw is presumably alleging then that Dahmer may have killed (or attacked at least) people while in Germany. There is no concrete evidence that this really happened though.

(709) One of the most notorious other necrophile serial killers was Jerry Brudos. Jerry Brudos was a serial killer who murdered four women in Oregon from 1968 to 1969. Brudos was a rapist and necrophile who killed because he couldn't control his foot fetish. He sawed off the foot of one victim and put in the freezer. He would then often take the foot out of the freezer and put ladies shoes on it. Jerry Brudos cut off the breasts of one of his victims so he could make plastic moulds with it. Jerry Brudos actually got married. It was said that he liked his wife to do the housework naked wearing nothing but a pair of high heeled shoes. Jerry Brudos was thankfully captured quite quickly. He died in prison in 2006. His prison cell was said to be full of ladies shoe catalogues when he died.

(710) Dahmer's attorney Wendy Patrickus said she felt like Clarice Starling in Silence of the Lambs when she first had to meet him.

(711) Necrophilia is commonly associated with those who suffer from depression and schizophrenia.

(712) Bridget Geiger said that when she went to the prom with Dahmer he hardly said a word to her all night.

(713) Dahmer's platoon leader during his army basic training said that Dahmer would usually leave the base on a Friday on his own. He was basically a complete loner.

(714) As far as serial killers go, Dahmer had a fairly normal childhood. It wasn't poverty stricken or rife with abuse. His parents got a fractious divorced but then many kids experience the same thing without going on to be serial killers.

(715) A lot of famous serial killers are found to have suffered from a head injury when they were young which (the theory goes) affected their mental state. There is no evidence though that this happened to Dahmer.

(716) Studies have shown that serial killers sometimes experience hallucinations about killing prior to the stage where they actually seek out victims.

(717) Dr. Park Dietz, the forensic psychiatrist who interviewed Dahmer, said that Dahmer was obsessed with Darth Vadar from Star Wars.

(718) Tracy Edwards said that as soon as he went in Dahmer's apartment, Dahmer put The Exorcist III on.

(719) Dahmer's platoon leader said he was a good learner during his basic training in the army.

(720) When Dahmer was visited by relatives in prison one of the first things he usually did was ask if the family cats were well.

(721) David Weinberger, whose son Jeremiah was killed by Jeffrey Dahmer, said he felt no satisfaction when he learned that Dahmer had been killed. He felt no sympathy for Dahmer but knew that nothing would bring his son back.

(722) Forensic psychiatrist Carl Wahlstrom, who interviewed Dahmer four times, said that Dahmer was never hesitant or reticent to talk about his crimes.

(723) Dahmer said that he tried to abstain from alcohol when he lived with his grandmother but he could never stick with

this for very long.

(724) Dennis Nilsen also strangled his victims like Dahmer. The crimes of these two men shared many uncanny similarities.

(725) Dahmer's stepmother said that Jeffrey Dahmer had curiously lifeless and dead eyes.

(726) Ted Bundy said that there were more serial killers than people think. He wasn't the first or last killer to say this.

(727) You can buy a Jeffrey Dahmer pillow case on Etsy.

(728) A blood stained saucepan was found in Dahmer's apartment when he was arrested.

(729) Killers like Dahmer lack the ability to think through the consequences of their actions. The fact that they are liable to end up in the electric chair or in prison for life never seems to factor into their thinking. They are too immersed in satisfying their compulsion to kill.

(730) Dahmer had a beloved dog named Frisky when he was a kid.

(731) Tracy Edwards said the most difficult thing about escaping from Dahmer was that Dahmer had eight locks on his door.

(732) John Backderf, who knew Jeffrey Dahmer at school and wrote the comic called My Friend Dahmer, said that an instinct told him not to forge a close friendship with Dahmer or ever see him out of school.

(733) Dahmer's parole-probation officer said he was always uncomfortable talking about his sexuality and would avoid the subject.

(734) Patrick Wayne Kearney was, like Dahmer, another notorious gay necrophile killer. Kearney was born in East Los Angeles in 1939. He confessed to 35 murders but the true figure is most likely considerably higher. Kearney is sometimes known as The Trash Bag Killer in true crime biographies. This is because he would dismember his victims into trash bags and dump them by the side of the road or put them in the desert.

He was not only a killer but a necrophile too. Kearney spent most of his spare time trawling the underbelly of the gay scene. His victims were mostly young men but he killed boys too. Kearney was only 5'5 tall and not the most physically imposing man. For this reason he used a gun and would shoot his victims dead while they were asleep or sitting in the car passenger seat next to him. He would then drive to a secluded spot and sexually abuse the body. Kearney said he would sometimes punch and kick the bodies of dead victims because he found this cathartic.

(735) Dahmer's stepmother said that he always hated any physical contact. He wasn't a hugging person that's for sure.

(736) Dahmer said that his murders escalated when he lost his job at the chocolate factory.

(737) Those who knew Dahmer said that he was monosyllabic when sober and only got chatty (to the point of tedium) when he was drunk.

(738) Those who knew Dahmer said he used to complain about rich people. Dahmer never had much money and this annoyed him. He felt life was unfair.

(739) Those who knew Dahmer in the army say that he occasionally made homophobic comments. This was clearly a calculated deflection to mask his own sexuality.

(740) Dahmer said he never had any friends after high school.

(741) John Backderf, who knew Dahmer at school and wrote the comic called My Friend Dahmer, said he joked to friends in 1988 that Jeffrey Dahmer was probably a serial killer by now.

(742) Dahmer said he only killed people he liked. If he hated you or didn't find you attractive then you were safe from him.

(743) Tracy Edwards had to punch Dahmer in the groin in order to escape.

(744) Serial killers don't really conform to any one method or strategy when it comes to getting rid of bodies. There are all sorts of methods killers use to get rid of bodies. The most effective is simply to dump them in a large river or the sea. Many killers in America leave the victims in a forest where a lot of decomposition will occur before they are found. Other killers (especially city dwellers) will just leave the bodies where they are - often because they love the thought of leaving a shocking crime scene. And then you get the killers like Dahmer and Nilsen who end up in a the nightmarish and surreal situation of living in a small apartment where the cupboards and drawers are full up with body parts, heads, and human flesh.

(745) Psychologytoday wrote of necrophilia - 'The need for an unrejecting partner is universal for most humans who desire an intimate relationship with another living human, as is the need to feel accepted. And so with necrophilia, it would be worth assessing all of the qualities people look for in a living person (using dating websites, and the ample pop psychology outlets), and seeing if those needs could be met with a deceased partner. A dead partner is not judgmental, there is no fear of needing to produce a reciprocal pleasure during sex, they cannot emotionally hurt anyone, they can be trusted, they do not answer back, there is no concern about offspring, and they can meet what is only a temporary need for sexual intimacy. The necrophiliac also has the luxury of creating, imagining, or fantasizing the corpse to be anything they want it to be.'

(746) Dahmer made about $25 a month in jail from cleaning the gym.

(747) Dahmer's defence team called him a 'steam-rolling killing machine' at the trial. They used language like this because their main task was to prove he was crazy.

(748) The police detectives who questioned Dahmer gave him muffins to eat.

(749) It is sometimes reported that Dahmer was beaten to death by a broom in prison but this isn't true. A broom with some blood on it (from the attack with a heavy weight from the gym) was found though.

(750) Dahmer apparently engaged in 'strangling games' with another boy when he was a kid.

(751) Dr Park Dietz, a prosecution witness at the trial, said that Dahmer had to drink before his murders to overcome his inhibitions about what he was doing.

(752) After Dahmer was battered to death in prison, a Republican politician named James Traficant created headlines when he said - "The truth is, Jeffrey Dahmer earned it, he deserved it."

(753) Two of the prosecution psychiatrists claimed that Dahmer might eventually have become successful in creating one of his 'zombiefied' sex slaves. Other psychiatrists involved in this case thought that was a ridiculous assertion.

(754) Dennis Nilsen, like Dahmer, also kept a victim's body in the shower/bath.

(755) Lionel Dahmer said he sobbed when he heard that his son had been killed in prison. He said his only comfort was knowing that 'Jeff' was now with his creator.

(756) Dahmer put a heavy metal door on his bedroom apartment to make it more secure than the rest of the apartment.

(757) Dahmer's fridge was amazingly tidy when the police opened it. All the body parts were neatly stacked and packaged.

(758) Dennis Nilsen, as he was with all serial killers, didn't seem comfortable when he was asked about Jeffrey Dahmer. It was like a threat to his identity in a sense - the fact that on the other side of the Atlantic was a man who had an almost identical MO and set of crimes (save for the cannibalism).

(759) Dahmer's mother Joyce said she telephoned her son once a week when he was in prison.

(760) It seems like everyone involved in the Dahmer case wrote a book about it. Even the minister who baptized him wrote a book about Dahmer. At one point, believe it or not, the judge in the trial was threatening to write a movie script about the Dahmer case.

(761) When he was in prison, an elderly nun once sent Dahmer some art books.

(762) Dahmer was rated as an 'average or slightly above average soldier' during his first year in the army.

(763) When he killed his first victim, Dahmer found the bones were too heavy to smash so he baked them in the oven to soften them up.
(764) Dahmer is sometimes called The Milwaukee Monster in true crime lore.

(765) Dahmer often worked at the chocolate factory six days a week.

(766) Dahmer was born at the Evangelical Deaconess Hospital

in Milwaukee.

(767) It was apparently Jeffrey Dahmer who chose the name David for his younger brother.

(768) Nikolai Espolovich Dzhumagaliev was another true crime cannibal. He was a Soviet serial killer who was convicted of seven murders committed from 1979 to 1980. He is known as Kolya the Maneater because he ate the flesh of some of his victims. Of his first murder, Dzhumagaliev told the police - "I cut the corpse's breast into strips, removed the ovaries, and separated the pelvis and hips; I then put these pieces into a backpack and carried them home. I melted the fat to fry with, and some parts I pickled. Once, I put the parts through a meat grinder and made dumplings. I saved the meat for myself; I never served it to anyone else. Twice, I grilled parts—the heart and the kidneys. Grilled meat, too. But it was tough, and I had to cook it for a long time in its own fat. The meat of this woman took me a month to eat. The first time I ate human flesh, I had to force myself, but then I got used to it."

(769) Dahmer's grandfather was a teacher.

(770) Jeffrey Dahmer said in prison that he didn't believe any person or intervention could have stopped him from killing people.

(771) What with his nightshift job and murderous necrophile activities, Dahmer barely got any sleep in the end.

(772) Dahmer said that killing people and doing as he pleased with their body was the only thing that ever gave him any satisfaction in life.

(773) Dahmer said he didn't especially enjoy feeling 'evil and perverted' but he simply couldn't control these sick desires and compulsions.

(774) Dahmer told an interviewer that he found killing

addictive.

(775) One of the problems with murderabillia items is that it is difficult to verify the authenticity of what you are buying.

(776) Shari Dahmer is played in the Netflix drama by Molly Ringwald. Molly Ringwald is forever associated with the 80s teen movies of John Hughes.

(777) It seems apparent that Dahmer's grandmother asked him to leave because she'd noticed that he kept bringing strange men back. One imagines she must have known in the end that her grandson was gay.

(778) In a prison interview, Dahmer was amused by the memory of the time he stole a mannequin and kept it in his bedroom.

(779) Dahmer's polaroids would show victims in various states of dismemberment. Dahmer seemed to like to chronicle his dissection.

(780) Dahmer seemed to be quite fond of shopping malls.

(781) Jeffrey Dahmer's mother Joyce apparently once saw a UFO and tried to follow it in her car.

(782) You could argue that John Backderf, who knew Jeffrey Dahmer at school and wrote a comic called My Friend Dahmer, was pretty mean to Dahmer. Backderf and friends treated Dahmer like some sort of performing monkey and plainly had no interest in being friends with him in the true sense.

(783) Dahmer told the police that he collected skulls because he considered skulls to represent the true essence of his victims.

(784) A neighbour of Dahmer said you never saw him with any

groceries or food shopping. The only thing he ever seemed to take into his apartment was beer.

(785) The 2018 horror film The Butchers features Jeffrey Dahmer and a number of other famous serial killers from history.

(786) Necrophilia is not associated with any one mental illness or disorder.

(787) When he was at school, Dahmer would call the alcohol he had his 'medicine'.

(788) Karl Denke is one of the most notorious cannibals in true crime besides Dahmer. Karl Denke was born in 1860 in the Kingdom of Prussia (now part of Poland). Denke is known as The Cannibal from Ziebice. Denke was well liked and an organist at the local Lutheran church. He had a small store which sold meat. He killed for the first time in 1903 by murdering a young slaughterhouse worker named Emma Sander (luckily for Denke, this murder was attributed to a wholly innocent man who had worked with the dead woman). The meat Denke sold in his shop was in reality the flesh of his victims. He was even a cannibal himself and sampled his own products. Denke usually pickled the meat of his victims and sold it in jars. It was clearly very popular because the shop did a flourishing trade.

Denke's gruesome exploits came to an end in 1924 when a homeless man went to the police to complain that a lunatic with an axe had just tried to murder him. When they investigated the workshop out the back of Denke's shop the police discovered that Denke had been making belts from human skin. He also used human hair to produce shoelaces. They also found huge piles of human bones and remains. These included 65 feet and metacarpal bones and 150 human ribs. There were bones from all parts of the human body and knives and axes all stained with blood.

(789) There is a theory that Dahmer suffered from Asperger syndrome.

(790) Dahmer's brother David is believed to have had two children.

(791) Police interviews with Dahmer amounted to around sixty hours of audiotape.

(792) A former detective and filmmaker have suggested that Dahmer might have murdered a young gay porn actor named William Newton in Los Angeles in 1990. Newton was last seen with a man who looked a lot like Dahmer. Dahmer denied this murder and there is no concrete evidence that he had anything to do with it. The theory as to why Dahmer would have denied this murder if he was guilty is presumably that California had the death penalty.

(793) Dahmer's mother Joyce was asked to write a book about her son but declined to do this.

(794) Jeremy Renner said he had no idea who Jeffrey Dahmer was before he played him in a 2002 movie.

(795) As we have noted, necrophilia is not rare at all in the most notorious true crime cases. It's a common theme in many serial killers. Gary Ridgway was born in 1949 in Salt Lake City, Utah. He is known as The Green River Killer and was convicted of 49 murders. The true kill count is almost certainly a lot higher than that figure. Ridgway, like many serial killers, targeted sex workers and teenage runaways and hitchhikers. Ridgway would usually strangle the victims and then sexually abuse the bodies - which he would leave in the woods and return to again. Gary Ridgway said he sometimes tried to bury victims as soon as he could because otherwise he was tormented by an insatiable urge to have sex with the corpses. Ted Bundy (by now captured) was consulted by the police when they were trying to solve the Green River Killer case. Bundy told the police that the killer probably returned to

burial sites to visit the bodies of his victims. He was certainly right about that.

(796) Dennis Nilsen was once asked if he had ever been tempted to eat his victims (like Jeffrey Dahmer did). He replied - "Oh, never, I'm strictly a bacon-and-eggs man."

(797) Radford University's 2016 report found that, on average, serial killers kill for the first time at 27 years-old. Dahmer was obviously much younger than this when he killed his first victim.

(798) Serial killers seem to have a superhuman ability to ignore foul odours. So many of them have lived in homes and apartments filled with body parts.

(799) It was incredibly disgusting that Dahmer's bed and mattress was covered in blood when he was captured. You'd think he would have made an attempt to clean it.

(800) Dahmer played the harmonica when he was a kid.

(801) The singer Lyfe Jennings claims he met Dahmer in prison. Jennings says that Dahmer said he was a fan of R&B music.

(802) The Reverend Jesse Jackson visited Milwaukee in the wake of Dahmer's capture. Jackson said of the Dahmer case - "It's a metaphor for all the social ills that plague our nation. Bad policing, underserved communities, the low value we assign to our young Black and brown men, especially if they happen to be gay."

(803) Dahmer said of his dead victims - "I could just lay around with them, without feeling pressure to do anything they wanted to do. They wouldn't make any demands on me. I could just enjoy them the way I wanted to."

(804) It is sometimes wrongly reported that Dahmer was

obsessed with Exorcist II: The Heretic. It was actually The Exorcist III. Exorcist II: The Heretic got famously bad reviews. William Friedkin, who made the original, called it the worst film he'd ever seen.

(805) Dahmer showed no emotion whatsoever in court when victim statements were read out and he was cursed and lunged at. He didn't even flinch.

(806) The relatives of Dahmer's victims got precious little in the way of compensation for the loss of their loved ones.

(807) Dahmer's death in prison seemed to most to have been very preventable. It was ridiculous that the most famous inmate in the prison and the one with the biggest target on his back was left unsupervised with a dangerous fellow prisoner.

(808) Dahmer found it very difficult when he was initially isolated in prison. He was essentially bored.

(809) After the trial verdict, Dahmer's grandmother put a sign on her door requesting that the media leave her alone.

(810) The prosecution was shrewd in the Dahmer trial because they told the jury they were not deciding if Dahmer was sane or insane. The prosecution suggested to the jury that if they had any doubt as to Dahmer's state of mind they would have to declare he was sane.

(811) Dahmer and Dennis Nilsen both had similar problems when it came to the stench of their apartments. There were a few incidents of neighbours complaining of a smell coming from Dennis Nilsen's 195 Melrose Avenue flat. Nilsen told them that the odour stemmed from structural problems in the building.

(812) A large number of criminals seem to 'find' God after being convicted. It is a way of trying to declare to the world that they have changed - even if they haven't in reality.

(813) Radford University's data suggested that over 50% of active serial killers are under 30.

(814) The press in Milwaukee thought the Shaker's Cigar Bar Cream City Cannibal tour (where you are shown around the old haunts of Jeffrey Dahmer) was rather distasteful.

(815) After the Dahmer trial had ended, the jury members said it had been a gruelling and harrowing experience to have to sit in court each day and listen to all the grim evidence concerning the monstrous and unfathomable things Dahmer had done.

(816) Dahmer was baptized in a prison infirmary whirlpool.

(817) Wendy Patrickus, who was one of Dahmer's lawyers, was only in her twenties when she represented Dahmer. It has been suggested in documentaries that her selection was very deliberate by the defence because to see Dahmer sitting next to a young attractive women in court made him seem less weird and scary.

(818) The police officer John Balcerzak made a joke on the police radio about needing to be 'deloused' after the tragic incident where Konerak Sinthasomphone was handed back to Dahmer.

(819) The illustration that Dahmer had drawn depicting the altar of skulls he planned to build was very childlike.

(820) Dahmer was specifically trained to be a medical specialist in the army. This is sort of like the military version of being an assistant to a nurse.

(821) Forensic psychiatrist Carl Wahlstrom, who interviewed Dahmer four times, said that Dahmer was obsessed with 'get rich quick' schemes.

(822) None of the psychiatric experts who evaluated Dahmer

before his trial judged that he was a racist.

(823) There was some degree of fear and controversy over Dahmer's insanity defence in that it was assumed that if it was successful and he went to a mental hospital rather than prison he'd stand a much better chance of being released one day. In reality though the institution he was sent to would have had no bearing on this. No one was ever going to put Jeffrey Dahmer back on the streets.

(824) Some viewers think there is a deliberate Jeffrey Dahmer lookalike in the background during a school scene in Stranger Things 4.

(825) Jeffrey Dahmer's autopsy cited the cause of death as multiple skull fractures and brain trauma.

(826) By the time it was decided to demolish Oxford Apartments, only fifteen people were still living in the building.

(827) When he was arrested, Dahmer told a psychiatrist that he'd had sexual relations with about a hundred men in the last five years.

(828) There was a solar eclipse the day that Dahmer was murdered.

(829) Dahmer's favourite TV show was apparently NYPD Blue. This was a cop drama show with Dennis Franz. Dahmer wouldn't have seen much of this show though because it only made its debut the year before he died.

(830) Dahmer apparently toyed with the idea of using electric shock treatment to create a zombie sex slave. He decided in the end though that he didn't have sufficient expertise to know how to do this.

(831) There is a lot of weird serial killer 'memorabilia' floating

around. Murderabilia products is the general term for these items. Some of this is available to buy and some of it has only been put on display in museums (of the macabre). Ebay banned the sale of serial killer artifacts on their sites in the end because they thought it was rather tasteless.

(832) Dahmer was said to be a fan of Star Trek.

(833) You can, should you desire, buy Jeffrey Dahmer fridge magnets on Etsy.

(834) The prison authorities originally believed that Dahmer might have been killed by a gang of inmates but they deduced it was simply Christopher Scarver acting alone.

(835) There were several different types of handsaw found in Damer's apartment.

(836) The computer that Dahmer had in his apartment was a Myoda.

(837) Wendy Patrickus, who was one of Dahmer's lawyers, said she had nightmares after interviewing Dahmer about his crimes.

(838) In a letter he wrote from prison, Dahmer said he was saving up to try and buy a word processor.

(839) Serial killers nearly always keep souvenirs from their crimes. Dahmer kept body parts, Bundy kept polaroids, and Joel Rifkin kept jewelry. Dennis Radar was was found to have a collection of driving licences belonging to his victims.

(840) A number of letters Dahmer got in prison were from highly disturbed people.

(841) When he was in prison, Dahmer got a lot of letters from religious people who wanted to understand him or try and save his soul.

(842) The chocolate factory where Dahmer worked was said to induce a wonderful sweet cocoa smell over the surrounding area.

(843) As part of his probation for sexual crimes, Dahmer had to attend a group therapy session. You probably won't be surprised to learn that, by all accounts, he barely spoke during the meeting.

(844) Soilex, which Dahmer used to boil heads, is more commonly used to remove wallpaper.

(845) Dahmer was said to smoke a lot of pot when he was a teenager.

(846) Ted Bundy said that after he killed a woman, he would sometimes shampoo their hair so they had less of an odour. There are no accounts of Dahmer doing this sort of thing.

(847) When he was captured and in custody, there were stories in the media that Dahmer had been granted special food and a television in his cell in return for telling the police everything about the murders.

(848) Dahmer went back to the remains of his first victim to dig them up after about two weeks. This was ostensibly to crush the bones but Dahmer's morbid fascination with dead bodies doubtless compelled him to go back.

(849) When it comes to disposing of bodies, serial killers vary. Some make an effort to get of evidence and some don't. It really depends on the circumstances of the murder and (in many cases) the intelligence (or indeed mental state) of the killer. A lot of serial killers leave the victims where they killed them and then flee the scene.

(850) The gay community in London were never happy with the way the Dennis Nilsen case was reported in the British tabloids. The tabloids often gave one the impression that the

gay community was rife with dangerous murderous predatory men preying on teenagers. There was a whiff of this sort of thing in the Dahmer case too although the possible racial subtext of Dahmer's victim selection was (rightly) equally salient in coverage.

(851) Dahmer's father did not show any emotion in court when the verdicts were read. He was internally shaken though and requested - and was granted - a moment alone with his son afterwards.

(852) Other killers who, like Jeffrey Dahmer, had thirteen letters in their name include Albert DeSalvo, Charles Manson, and Aileen Wuornos.

(853) Gerald Boyle had already represented Dahmer in various cases before Dahmer was revealed to be a serial killer. Boyle knew Dahmer was troubled but he'd never suspected that 'Jeff' was capable of murder.

(854) Dahmer said he ate the piece of human bicep because he was intrigued by how large it was.

(855) The Cream City Cannibal Jeffery Dahmer Walking Tour, where you are guided around Dahmer's old haunts, costs about $80 to go on.

(856) It has been estimated in some studies that only around 22% of serial killers use firearms when they kill. Dahmer never used a firearm to murder anyone.

(857) Tracy Edwards said that Dahmer threatened to cut his heart out before he (thankfully) managed to escape.

(858) There were only seats available for 23 reporters at Dahmer's trial. The media demand was much higher than this.

(859) Jeffrey Dahmer said he could never find any meaning in his life.

(860) John A. Balcerzak and Joseph P. Gabrish, the police officers who handed the dazed and confused victim Konerak Sinthasomphone back to Jeffrey Dahmer and certain death, didn't even bother to ask for identification to establish old Konerak Sinthasomphone really was. They also failed to take much of a look inside Dahmer's apartment. The two police officers just seemed to want to wash their hands of this affair and leave.

(861) Dahmer told John A. Balcerzak and Joseph P. Gabrish that Konerak Sinthasomphone's name was John Hmong.

(862) It is a common trait in many serial killers that they used prostitutes before they became killers. This is another serial killer trope though that didn't apply to Dahmer.

(863) Those who knew Dahmer at school say he could chug a six pack of beer in a matter of minutes.

(864) When Dahmer's mother left home with her younger son David, Lionel Dahmer was away so the teenage Jeffrey Dahmer was left alone for a time with no food in the house. This is speculated to have left him with abandonment issues.

(865) Those who rememered Dahmer from his gay nightclub days say he was a good looking man.

(866) Radford University described Dahmer as an 'organised lust' type of serial killer.

(867) John Backderf, who knew Jeffrey Dahmer at school and wrote a comic called My Friend Dahmer, said he was at a house only yards away when Dahmer's first murder was taking place. He obviously only found about this years later.

(868) Dahmer was mentioned in a Mac Miller song.

(869) Dahmer was apparently thinking about doing a business major at college.

(870) Three potential victims in all managed to escape from Dahmer.

(871) When he was at college living at Morril Tower, Dahmer lived in a male only section called Ross House.

(872) The kids at school thought Dahmer was weird because he had a briefcase. The briefcase was where Dahmer stashed his booze.

(873) Bridget Geiger, who went to the prom with Dahmer, said that at the time she thought he was basically a good kid and felt a bit sorry for him.

(874) Dahmer's platoon leader during his army basic training said that, unlike the other recruits, Dahmer rarely got any mail.

(875) Dahmer's mother knew he was gay and didn't care. She accepted his sexuality.

(876) Earle Nelson was one of the first necrophile killers to become well known. Earle Nelson was born in 1897 in San Francisco, California. He tends to be known as The Dark Strangler. Earle was the first prolific American serial killer of the 20th century (indeed for many years he thought to be the MOST prolific American serial killer - at least until the serial killer explosion of later years). Nelson's killing spree began in 1926. His modus operandi soon became clear. Nelson would dress him quite smartly and, Bible in hand, pretend to be a Christian traveller looking for a room to rent. His targets were middle-aged landladies. Once he had charmed the landlady sufficiently and got his foot inside the door (so to speak), Nelson would strangle them (sometimes with a chord) and then usually have sex with the body. He is credited with 22 murders but there are at least seven unsolved murders where he is considered to be a suspect.

(877) One of Dahmer's pranks in high school was to make

sheep like noises in class.

(878) There appears to be ample evidence that Dahmer owned an electric saw. No prizes for guessing what this was used for.

(879) David Rodriguez shared a room with Dahmer when they did their basic training for the army. Rodriguez later told the media that Dahmer was a 'gin-swilling wimp' who never showed much interest in anything. Rodriguez was pretty shocked that the meek unassuming person he remembered was now the most notorious serial killer in the world.

(880) Alexander Bychkov was a Russian serial killer who killed nine men from 2009 to 2012. In his confession to the police, Bychkov claimed that he ate livers, hearts and the muscle of his victims. Bychkov drew comparisons to Dahmer in the Russian media.

(881) Dahmer does not appear to have been one of those serial killers who kept personal items (like ID, jewelry etc) belonging to his victims. He was more interested in body parts and bones. There were a few victim driving licences in his apartment though when he was captured.

(882) Army colleagues said that Dahmer would get drunk on martinis in his bunk when he had some free time.

(883) Dahmer was apparently quite a sickly child and always picking up ear and throat infections.

(884) There was a murder near the Ohio State campus while Dahmer was a student there. The police later retrospectively investigated this murder again (in the wake of Dahmer's capture) but concluded that the campus murder had no connection to Dahmer.

(885) One of Dahmer's college roomates got moved to other accommodation because he was unhappy about Dahmer's heavy drinking.

(886) Dahmer got $10 each time he donated blood and plasma at college. He desperately needed this money to fund his drinking.

(887) Dahmer is alleged to have stolen a radio, watch, and $100 from the rooms of fellow college students while they were at a party.

(888) It would probably be fair to say the young Dahmer was completely directionless. He was perfectly happy to drink and watch TV all day and didn't really think about the future. It was a very day to day sort of existence.

(889) A student who went to Ohio State college in 1998 said there was sign on the door of Dahmer's old room which read - "Yes, Jeffrey Dahmer used to live here. No, you cannot come in to see it."

(890) Attempts to connect Dahmer to unsolved murders in Germany never really went anywhere because most of the murders were of women and that definitely wasn't Nielsen's MO.

(891) When he was captured, Dahmer waived his right to have a lawyer present throughout his questioning.

(892) The special 'altar' that Dahmer planned to construct was going to have two full skeletons at the front and then the shrunken heads of other victims in the background. Suffice to say, Dahmer was completely crazy by this point.

(893) Dahmer said he regretted killing David Thomas because he wasn't even that attracted to him. Dahmer did not keep any bones or body parts of this victim.

(894) Dahmer's father maintained that his son could have been 'cured' if he'd been sent to a mental hospital.

(896) Dahmer smoked menthol cigarettes.

(897) Eminem and The Manic Street Preachers are among the artists who have mentioned Jeffrey Dahmer in songs.

(898) Billy Capshaw, the army medic who says Dahmer abused him in Germany, later worked in a nursing home and served some time in prison for negligent homicide. Capshaw said he telephoned Dahmer once after they'd left the army but that Dahmer was indifferent and had no real interest in talking to him.

(899) One of the famous necrophiles in all true crime is Carl Tanzler. Carl Tanzler was born in Dresden in 1877. He went by a battery of other names though and liked to pretend he was a relative of Countess von Cosel. Tanzler went to Australia as a youngish man but when the First World War broke out he was interned by the authorities there. He eventually went back to Germany where he got married married and had two daughters. Tanzler was quite an eccentric man but he seemed harmless enough. One of his great hobbies was working on inventions. He was always trying to build boats or things of that nature.

In 1926, Tanzler moved to the United States. He had some relatives in Zephyrhills, Florida, so ended up here. His wife and daughters later joined him but he eventually left them and took a job as a radiology technician at the U.S. Marine Hospital in Key West. The details on why Tanzler became estranged from his wife and daughters are vague but it seems safe to say that his state of mind and grasp on reality became increasingly frayed when they were no longer with him. Tanzler was plainly someone who had a difficult relationship with reality. He was plagued with visions of Countess von Cosel from a young age and these visions had shown him a glimpse of a darkly beautiful woman who he believed he was destined to meet and fall in love with.

Fate was to intervene at this point and unwittingly feed the delusions of Tanzler in unforunate fashion. At the hospital where Tanzler worked, a twenty-two year woman named

Maria Elena Milagro de Hoyos was brought for medical tests because of ill health. Elena was darkly attractive and Tanzler was instantly smitten. In fact, he was convinced that Maria Elena Milagro de Hoyos was the woman he had seen in his childhood visions. Panzler believed it was no accident that Elena had ended up in the hospital where he worked. He believed this was destiny and that Elena was supposed to be the love of his life.

It transpired though that Elena had tuberculosis - which was a serious and fatal condition at the time. Tanzler was devastated. He took it upon himself to try and save her life - despite the fact that he wasn't even a doctor. He concocted potions and quack remedies and even used electrodes on Elena in the faint hope that it might cure her. Tanzler showered her with gifts and seemed determined to keep her spirits up. Elena's family presumably thought it was a bit odd that this radiologic technician was taking such an interest but he was clearly persuavive and trustworthy and they were probably grateful for any medical help at all given the gravity of the situation. As it turned out though,

Tanzler's various attempts to cure Elena were purely speculative and had no chance of success. He was simply deluding himself and Elena's family. His amateurish and eccentric crackpot medical efforts were predictably all to no avail and she died on October 25, 1931. Tanzler offered to pay for Elena's funeral and her family (who didn't have much money) seemed happy to accept this kind and generous offer. Tanzler arranged for her body to put in a mausoleum but - unknown to Elena's family - Carl Tanzler was the only person with a key to this tomb. Tanzler visited Elena's tomb each and every day. He brought flowers and even had a telephone installed in the tomb - a move which obviously suggested his mental health was not on the most firm footing. Over the years which followed there was increasing local speculation in the community about Tanzler's eccentric behaviour. It was said that he had become reclusive and was sometimes seen buying women's clothes and perfume. You can probably see where this story is heading can't you? Suffice to say, there was something of Norman Bates in Carl Tanzler. In the end a rather macabre rumour began to circulate in the area. The rumour was that Tanzler was living with Elena's corpse. Elena's sister Florinda got wind of this rumour and decided there was only one thing to do. She would have to go and visit Tanzler to find out the truth for herself. When she arrived at the house she saw Tanzler dancing with Elena's corpse through the window. Florinda called the police and Tanzler's disturbing secret life was secret no more. It transpired that Tanzler had stolen Elena's body from the tomb about two years after her death.

He had used a trolley to take it home (this was presumably done in the dead of night when there would be few people around). Before that Tanzler would visit the tomb each day and said that Elena's ghost would visit him to sing songs. He claimed that Elena's ghost instructed him to take the body home. When he took home the corpse he kept Elena in a laboratory and when the skin decomposed he replaced it with wax and plaster of paris. He used coat hangers and wires to maintain the posture of the body and stuffed it with rags. He also put glass eyes in the corpse. Panzler used perfumes and disinfectant to mask the smell. He would sit and have dinner with the corpse each night and talk to it as if it was a living person. He is believed to have slept next to the corpse in his bed although whether he tried to have sex with it is open to question. Some accounts say he did and some say he didn't. It's probably safe to say that Tanzler was crazy. He said he had plans to build an aircraft on which he would launch Elena into the atmosphere. He believed the heat and radiation would then magically bring her back to life. Surprisingly, Tanzler was deemed fit to stand trial. The charges were obviously for destroying a grave and stealing a body. There wasn't though much anger at Tanzler for his actions. Most people seemed to feel sorry for him. Though his actions were macabre many felt he was just a lonely eccentric. The authorities dropped the charges in the end and seemed to have no appetite for punishing him. Tanzler was not a murderer or an evil man. He was a deeply troubled man who taken to graverobbing because of a romantic obsession with a woman who was no longer alive. Elena was buried in an unmarked grave (lest Panzler should track down her body again) and this strange case was put in the past. Tanzler died in 1952. It is said that he built himself a life sized doll of Elena to live with and died in the doll's arms.

(900) In 2022, a young English woman named Britnee Chamberlain created some controversy by revealing she had a Jeffrey Dahmer tattoo on her lower leg. The phrase "if you can't beat 'em, eat 'em" was alongside Dahmer's picture. Britnee also seemed to have a tatto of Ted Bundy. "I don't condone the hostile crimes of serial killers by any means. I am simply intrigued as to why they do it," she said.

(901) Dahmer victim Tony Hughes had been friends with Dahmer for two years when he was murdered.

(902) When he was captured, Dahmer had no food in his apartment but he did have several condiments. There was also a big jar of mustard.

(903) Dahmer told his father that prison food was really awful.

(904) Some early warning signs that someone might become a killer are alleged to be bed wetting, starting fires, a dysfunctional relationship with one or both parents, and childhood abuse. Jeffery Dahmer experienced none of these.

(905) Jeffrey Dahmer was far from the first killer to use acid to dispose of victims. John George Haigh was a British serial killer known as the Acid Bath Murderer. Haigh was basically a thief and conman who became inspired by the tale of Georges-Alexandre Sarret, a French killer who used sulphuric acid to dispose of victims. Haigh was hung in 1949.

(906) There has been a serial killer board game - which naturally created some controversy.

(907) We seem to be completely obsessed by serial killers. You can find a documentary about one on TV most nights.

(908) In his police confession, Jeffrey Dahmer said that he was dissolving bodies in a vat of acid because he had run out of money and feared he would be thrown out of his apartment. He wanted to destroy all evidence of his crimes before this happened.

(909) The FBI generally states that one must kill three people to qualify as a serial killer. There must also be a gap between each killing (a bomber, for example, is a mass murderer or terrorist as opposed to a serial killer).

(910) One other theory for the reduction in American serial killers in recent years is that the parole system has changed and there are longer sentences. There is less chance of a dangerous individual being released.

(911) According to some true crime sites, Dahmer had a higher IQ than either Ted Bundy or Harold Shipman. Harold Shipman was the infamous British doctor who murdered hundreds of his patients with morphine.

(912) Dahmer was a fan of the band Motley Crue.

(913) When he was in prison, Dahmer got some nutty letters from racists and Nazis congratulating him for killing black people.

(914) When he was captured and sent to prison, Dahmer was put on suicide watch after a razor blade was found hidden in his cell.

(915) Lionel Dahmer said that when his son became infamous he occasionally got crank calls on his answerphone making bad taste Jeffery Dahmer jokes.

(916) Dahmer owned a copy of The Satanic Bible as a young

man. The Satanic Bible is a collection of essays, observations, and rituals published by Anton LaVey in 1969.

(917) Dahmer was addicted to the power he felt when he had mastery of a dead person. He was acting out his darkest fantasy. The fantasy could never be permanent though. The bodies would inevitably decay and smell. They had to be disposed of. Dahmer then had to kill again to begin the fantasy afresh. It was what you might describe as a classic example of a vicious circle.

(918) Dahmer wanted to use wire to make complete skeletons of some of his victims but he never got around to this.

(919) We don't actually know how much human flesh Dahmer ate. Dahmer initially told the police he had done this once but then conceded he'd done it more than once. He could have eaten human flesh dozens of times for all we know.

(920) When he purchased the infamous freezer for his apartment, Dahmer told his family that he'd bought so he could stock up on sale items and save money.

(921) As we have noted, there are various conflicting theories as to why Dahmer killed mostly black men. It could have been a sexual preference (though Dahmer allegedly said in prison his ideal boyfriend would be white), it could have been because he lived in a mostly black area, or it could have been because Dahmer deemed that black victims would have been less likely to be reported in the media or attract the attention of the police. Another possibility sometimes mentioned is the fact that the gay community was very diverse and so Dahmer simply encountered a very eclectic range of people when he went out to gay bars and clubs.

(922) Dahmer often kept his disturbing polaroid photographs of victims in a blue briefcase. Some were found in a drawer too.

(923) Dahmer's apartment was, given the circumstances, remarkably tidy when he was captured.

(924) Dahmer requested that there should be no funeral or grave after his death.

(925) Tracy Edwards, the man who fatefully escaped from Dahmer, was later accused of both sexual assault of a minor and participation in a murder. He has served some prison time and is believed to be homeless.

(926) Dahmer doesn't appear to have been a serial killer who tortured his victims. He basically just wanted them dead.

(927) The tension between fantasy and reality is sometimes cited as a big factor in the pyschology of serial killers like Dahmer. Serial killers seem detached from reality. They are overpowered by their dark fantasies and attempt to make fantasy a part of reality.

(928) Dahmer was sentenced to eight years in 1989 for 2nd degree assault but only served ten months.

(929) Dahmer said he threw the stolen mannequin away because his grandmother found it and thought it was a weird thing to have.

(930) Dahmer was a fan of the band Black Sabbath.

(931) One of Dahmer's first part-time jobs as a kid was in a nursery selling plants.

(932) Dahmer was very fond of one of his teachers at Hazel Harvey Elementary School and once brought her in some tadpoles as a gift.

(933) Dahmer's drunk and disorderly incidents indicate that he could be a violent drunk.

(934) The high school that Dahmer went to has a 'hall of fame' which features notable and successful people who went there. You probably won't be surprised to learn that Dahmer doesn't feature.

(935) Lionel Dahmer said he was 'dumbfounded' when he learned his son was a serial killer. He had always considered his son to be a kind person.

(936) One could argue that Dahmer should have been caught much earlier. All the cops needed to do was search his car after the first murder or his apartment after the Konerak Sinthasomphone incident and Dahmer would have exposed.

(937) The judge who sentenced Christopher Scarver for killing Dahmer said that Scarver must not be allowed to become a 'folk hero' for his actions.

(938) Dennnis Nilsen was said to be highly irritated when Jeffrey Dahmer became much more famous than him.

(939) In his book, Lionel Dahmer said that, like his son, he had sometimes had dark thoughts and desires but he was able to suppress these thoughts and focus on his work and healthy normal things.

(940) The banality of evil is a phrase that could have been invented purely for Jeffrey Dahmer. Court reporters at the trial were shocked at how dull and ordinary he was in the flesh.

(941) Dahmer had weekly Bible study in prison.

(942) Dahmer had trouble making friends his whole life. He was a very withdrawn and shy sort of person who kept people at arm's length.

(943) One of the most remarkable things about Dahmer is that he managed to live in that apartment with the stench of death

and decay in his nostrils. He must have built up some sort of immunity to withstand that odour.

(944) The photographs found in Dahmer's apartment suggested he had a particular fascination and kink about male chests.

(945) Dahmer would sometimes pull the intestines out of his dead victims. He found this sexually exciting.

(946) Dahmer was said to have a particular dislike for the television chat show Geraldo.

(947) When he was in the army, Dahmer was stationed in Baumholder. Baumholder is a town in the Birkenfeld district in Rhineland-Palatinate, Germany, in the Westrich, an historic region that encompasses areas in both Germany and France.

(948) Christopher Scarver, who was black, was allegedly not too fond of white people so it could be (according to one theory) that his murder of Dahmer was revenge for Dahmer mostly killing black people. It should be noted that the police did not support this theory.

(949) Dahmer would usually have a bottle of Bailey's Irish Cream in his apartment.

(950) Dahmer said he would target victims who were alone. If he saw someone with a group of friends he knew it would be too risky.

(951) Dahmer told the police that he'd always lived in a little private world of his own and he'd grown to enjoy this.

(952) Dahmer's college education was doomed right from the start because he rarely attended any classes due to his drinking.

(953) Studies have shown that necrophilic serial killers like

Dahmer are much more likely to mutilate and cut up the victims.

(954) Dahmer was a big dinosaur buff as a kid. This was one of the few things he had in common with his brother.

(955) Dahmer seemed to be fond of rum. He had this in common with Dennis Nilsen.

(956) A study once claimed that a serial killer's method of murder is related to IQ. A smart killer will use a gun while a stupid one will be more bestial and basic. This study doesn't make perfect sense because killers with fairly high IQs like Dahmer, Kemper, and Bundy, were amongst the most gruesome killers. Aileen Wuornos, who was no rocket scientist, always used a gun.

(957) Dahmer had a copy of the film Blade Runner in his apartment when he was arrested.

(958) Dahmer spent a lot of time on cleaning duties in prison. He must have been sick of mops in the end.

(959) The pastor who baptized Dahmer in prison lost a lot of his church members as a consequence of this controversial act.

(960) Dahmer took a class in administrative law at college.

(961) Dahmer owned an Ouija board when he was a teenager.

(962) Some of the True Crime collectible sites sell a transcript of Jeffrey Dahmer's police confession. However, you can download this in PDF form for free if you look around.

(963) Our enduring fascination with serial killers stems from the fact that they are completely unfathomable and alien to us. We are constrained in our actions by compassion, guilt, remorse, empathy, and kindness. Most of us are very squeamish. Serial killers are not constrained by any of these

emotions. They rape, torture, kill and commit the most gruesome acts as if it was the most natural thing in the world.

(964) When he was arrested, Dahmer was asked if he thought he could ever have a normal life if he was released one day. Dahmer replied that he'd go straight back to killing people if anyone was ever stupid enough to release him.

(965) The older you are the less chance you have of being killed by a serial killer. There are exceptions of course but serial killers (when given a choice) generally tend to target very young victims.

(966) A true crime collectible site put up for sale an Ambrosia chocolate factory paycheck made out to Jeffrey Dahmer. Dahmer's signature is on the back. The price you'd have to pay to own this paycheck? $15,000!

(967) Jeffrey Dahmer was a Gemini.

(968) Dahmer may have appeared alarmingly 'normal' and placid in his interviews but his Vulcan like lack of emotion was definitely chilling.

(969) Dahmer was a big fan of the Clive Barker horror movie Hellraiser.

(970) The police found a Bible in Dahmer's apartment when he was arrested.

(971) When he was arrested Dahmer had a bag of human flesh in his freezer that he'd never been able to move because it was stuck to the ice.

(972) Dahmer liked Budweiser beer.

(973) Dahmer had Odosorb in his apartment when he was arrested. Odosorb is an odour-neutralising concentrate.

(974) When he was a boy, Jeffrey Dahmer would play with animal bones he found in the woods and under the porch.

(975) Though he was quite good looking as a teen, Dahmer said that girls never took an interest in him.

(976) Dahmer was a fan of The Beatles.

(977) The forensic psychiatrist Dr. Park Elliott Dietz was one of the people who argued that Dahmer was not insane. Dietz pointed out that Dahmer, in an era of AIDs, had always practiced safe sex and avoided any risk. This, argued Dietz, was not the action of an insane person.

(978) Lionel Dahmer donated proceeds from his book about his son to the famalies of the victims. The relatives of Dahmer's victims held no ill will towards Lionel Dahmer. They knew he was a decent man who wasn't to blame for what Jeffery Dahmer did.

(979) In 1992, Hart Fisher published a comic book titled Jeffery [sic] Dahmer: An Unauthorized Biography Of A Serial Killer. The comic was, as you might imagine, highly controversial and drew complaints from the relatives of Dahmer's victims. The distributor of the comic even destroyed a lot of them at one point. Fisher even went on the Jerry Springer show at one point to defend the comic.

(980) Dahmer said that by eating the flesh of his victims this made it feel like they had come alive again in him.

(981) Dahmer had an audio cassette on Creation Science in his apartment when he was arrested.

(982) The jury at the Dahmer trial were not allowed to watch television, use the telephone, read newspapers, or discuss the case with anyone outside court. It was somewhat easier in those days to avoid the news because there were no cell phones, social media, or internet.

(983) 34 seats were were reserved at Dahmer's trial for the relatives of the victims.

(984) Dahmer wrote a long letter to read at the trial. Part of it read - "Your Honor: It is now over. This has never been a case of trying to get free. I didn't ever want freedom. Frankly, I wanted death for myself. This was a case to tell the world that I did what I did, but not for reasons of hate. I hated no one. I knew I was sick or evil or both. Now I believe I was sick. The doctors have told me about my sickness, and now I have some peace.. I know how much harm I have caused...Thank God there will be no more harm that I can do. I believe that only the Lord Jesus Christ can save me from my sins...I ask for no consideration."

(985) Raising Jeffrey Dahmer is a 2006 film which has Rusty Sneary as Dahmer. The film is about Dahmer's relationship with his father.

(986) Dahmer's attorney Gerald P. Boyle said at the trial that Jeffrey Dahmer was not evil but merely sick.

(987) The 1995 Joyce Carol Oates novel Zombie is based on Dahmer. The novel is about a serial killer who tries to create a zombified sex slave.

(988) Dahmer's father Lionel was a regular at his trial. He was usually mobbed by the media when he made his way into the building.

(989) The Milwaukee Police Department expanded their patrols in the wake of the Dahmer case in an attempt to make the local community feel safer.

(990) Anne E Schwartz is a journalist who broke the Dahmer story. She actually got to look inside his apartment after he was arrested. Schwartz said that Dahmer's apartment seemed surprisingly normal. It didn't look like the chaotic squalid home of a depraved killer.

(991) Dahmer's mother Joyce was later a case manager at the Central Valley AIDS Team and founder of "The Living Room," an HIV community center that opened in Fresno in 1996. When she died she was described by those that knew her as a kind and wonderful person.

(992) There is no evidence that Dahmer was inspired by any other killer or had any particular interest in true crime.

(993) Dahmer was banned from the bathouse he frequented after it came to light that he'd been drugging people.

(994) Those who worked in the prison say that Christopher Scarver's claims that Dahmer taunted other prisoners about his crimes are complete nonsense.

(995) Dahmer was baptized in prison on the same day that the notorious serial killer John Wayne Gacy was executed.

(996) Dahmer said he planned to sit at the alter of skulls in a leather chair.

(997) Dahmer's cremation only happened a year after his death because of the debate over what to do with his brain. Dahmer's parents got half of his ashes each.

(998) The army paid for Dahmer's ticket to Florida. After his discharge they offered to pay the travel expenses for wherever he wanted to go.

(999) During his police confession, Dahmer said - "It's hard for me to believe that a human being could have done what I've done, but I know that I did it."

(1000) The last thing ever eaten by Dahmer before he was killed in prison was a toasted cheese sandwich. This was a very run of the mill last meal for one of history's most notorious cannibals.